The Vertical Labyrinth

Marie-Louise von Franz, Honorary Patron

**Studies in Jungian Psychology
by Jungian Analysts**

Daryl Sharp, General Editor

The
Vertical
Labyrinth

Individuation in Jungian Psychology

Aldo Carotenuto

Translated by John Shepley

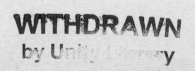

Originally published in Italian as *Il labirinto verticale*.
Copyright © 1981 Casa Editrice Astrolabio.

Canadian Cataloguing in Publication Data

Carotenuto, Aldo
   The vertical labyrinth

(Studies in Jungian psychology by Jungian analysts; 20)

Translation of: Il labirinto verticale.

Includes bibliographical references and index.

ISBN 0-919123-19-8.

1. Psychoanalysis - Case studies.   2. Jung,
C. G. (Carl Gustav), 1875-1961.   I. Title.
II. Series.

RC509.8.C3713 1985   616.89′17′0926   C85-098014-3

INNER CITY BOOKS
Box 1271, Station Q, Toronto, Canada M4T 2P4
Telephone (416) 927-0355

Honorary Patron: Marie-Louise von Franz.
Publisher and General Editor: Daryl Sharp.
Editorial Board: Fraser Boa, Daryl Sharp, Marion Woodman.

INNER CITY BOOKS was founded in 1980 to promote the
understanding and practical application of the work of C.G. Jung.

Cover: The labyrinth or maze, traditional symbol of the path
of life, can represent a crucial moment in the journey of
self-knowledge, a point when the archetype of the hero
is constellated (see text, pages 48ff).

Index by Daryl Sharp

Printed and bound in Canada by Webcom Limited

Contents

See final pages for descriptions of other INNER CITY BOOKS

The goal is important only as an idea; the
essential thing is the *opus* [the work on oneself]
which leads to the goal: *that* is the goal of a lifetime.
—C.G. Jung, *The Practice of Psychotherapy*

1

The Mythical Unconscious

The man whose story I tell here is a successful painter who for six years shared with me some moments of his life. Now that the memory is distant, and the turbulent images of his sufferings form a background to many other experiences with which my work is filled, the outlines of an inner life and the discrepancy between existence and being appear more clearly to my mind. Perhaps every patient, should one care to lower one's gaze into the depths of neurotic torment, finds himself in the position of having to deny himself in order to be able to live. Juvenal summed up this position in the line, *"Et, propter vitam, vivendi perdere causas"* (To lose what gives life its value for the sake of saving your skin).[1]

Fame pursued this man, but strangely enough this success was completely separate from the feeling he had about himself. For some time he had been troubled by the suspicion that he was dissembling, that he was not, so to speak, up to the situation. Glory and artistic recognition seemed to him an extraneous excrescence on his inner reality, and the only way to deal with this distressing feeling was complete inactivity. He would, of course, have liked to go on painting, but the block was total: a sad farewell to creativity, a wish for death, the tragic and painful confrontation with his own failure.

This is a sufficiently common experience that can strike anyone, man or woman, particularly at certain fundamental moments of existence. Perhaps it could also be called fear, but a special kind of fear, without well-defined outlines and endowed with almost mysterious characteristics, paralyzing in part and in part propelling. It is a fear that has to do with the world and with our own being in the face of it. But the world is infinite and gives us no response. As Spengler writes: "The birth of the Ego, and of the world-anxiety with which it is identical, is one of the final secrets of humanity and of mobile life generally."[2]

When he is seated in front of me, I know that his fear may be the beginning of a new life even though it appears in the guise of the tragic, in which he could end by losing himself. On the other hand, there are no simpler alternatives in these situations. A rapid, and above all certain, solution of our emotional blocks is everybody's dream, but unfortunately it remains for the moment an unfulfilled wish.

Arion, as I shall call him, had heard of me, and even before our meeting (for the simple reason that someone had suggested psychological analysis to him as the only possibility for recovery) he has begun to experience me as a powerful and accomplished person. At that moment he has an absolute need to believe that I am omnipotent, to think that I have understood more than what I say and write. His need to see me in this light stems from the fact that, like anyone in a psychological crisis, he has lost his capacity to make decisions and is in his turn governed by impulses that do not pass through thought but discharge themselves immediately under the impact of external stimuli. His deepest wish is that I, thanks to my power, should be able to tell him what to do, that is, suggest to him the way to be happy. This is the greatest mistake people make about analytic therapy, for in reality it has nothing to do with making anyone happy. The analyst's concern is a more modest one, and that is to help the patient to, in Jung's words, "acquire steadfastness and philosophic patience in face of suffering."[3] I leave him in his illusion but at the same time I am obliged, in the face of his devastated life, to take account of myself, to make an honest reckoning of my own existence. Jung himself made the fundamental observation that "we meet ourselves time and again in a thousand disguises on the path of life."[4]

It is difficult for people to understand that it is possible to help someone else only if his or her fate touches us, even if only marginally. This new patient pushes me toward my own "cosmic fear," which I, perhaps distracted by the sounds of daily life, persist in not hearing. Or else by his mere presence he may indicate to me the points where I have failed or might fail, where I have foundered without realizing it. And so the patient is not only a clinical "case," that term so dear to the medical, so-called scientific profession. He is something more, and has to be something more because otherwise I would have no possibility of understanding him.

I must also say that at certain moments in our time together I had the feeling of working psychologically only for myself, but in reality what I was offering my patient was not exactly insignificant. To his destruction I was opposing something different. If he could infect me with his neurosis, I could offer him the contagion of my "presumed" sanity. If he was blocked, I was not, but I was well aware of what it means to be blocked. I leave myself open to him completely and allow him to fill my unconscious with his illness, but I too will fill him with my own contents. As Jung says: "Doctor and patient thus find themselves *in a relationship founded on mutual unconsciousness.*"[5]

And so the fact is that my understanding has passed through my own suffering and been filtered by the comparison with my personal situation. Every true analysis has this characteristic, and if it is missing it is not an analysis but a benevolent relationship in the course of which, if things go well, a modest strengthening of the conscious situation is achieved. And if there are analysts who state the contrary, they are lying and know they are lying: this is actually a defensive attitude taken against the direct impact of the other, an impact involving deep and serious problems since sooner or later the most scabrous and painful things in our experience come to light. But this path is necessary for psychological rebirth.

The notion of psychological rebirth confronts us with the problem of the development of consciousness. Of course, the man of a hundred thousand years ago did not have the same kind of consciousness that we have today, and we must suppose that a gradual process of development allowed man at a certain moment to put to himself the first and fundamental question: who am I? This possibility of self-interrogation coincides with a radical transformation: man's existence emerges from a purely natural dimension and acquires "human" quality. I cannot say whether we should be proud of this event, but the fact remains that it was by putting this question to ourselves that we began to write history.

This same model of evolution can be traced in the life of each of us, which is to say that if with suitable instruments we examine our psychic development on the ontogenetic plane, we can recognize in it the same phases that characterize the phylogenetic process followed by all humanity. It is not by chance that I say "suitable instruments," since awareness always depends on them. Analysis is doubtless an instrument, but it is important to note that, to the extent that it traces the psychic structuring of the individual exclusively to his personal history, it is merely reductive and is not capable of offering that broad range of results and cultural data peculiar instead to an analysis carried on in light of the transpersonal or archetypal. Indeed, it is sometimes possible to deal with psychological discomfort without at all leading it back to the ontogenetic and personalistic dimension, but by referring solely to those "mythical" models that mark the stages of psychological development both in the individual and in mankind.[6]

But what is the connection between mythology, psychology and human suffering? One might say that a link between mythical tales and human vicissitudes has always been perceived, but only the instruments of analysis have offered the possibility of making these connections obvious and operative for the awareness of modern man. Even before writing delivered to men their own history, the oral tradition delivered the myth, by which man tried to interpret and explain what was happening in the world. Myth, in this view, is a way of responding to the apparent absurdity of existence. That is to say, it brings order to chaos and forms the first nucleus of what will later be the *meaning* of life.

The meaning of life, however, coincides neither with the truth nor with reality. Analysts ought always to be aware of this limitation and should also understand that to "interpret" signifies only to impart meaning to an apparent chaos. Starting then from this presupposition, it is possible at every harsh and painful moment experienced by the patient who sits before us to recognize something that has already essentially been said, but which now clothes itself in a new history. In this way we perform an operation of universalization that removes the suffering patient from the sense of absurdity and meaninglessness and places him in a context of ties, references and allusions whose therapeutic power is beyond measure. Myths were developed during the course of history, and an examination of them permits us to see the development of consciousness in all its stages. Thus one can rightly say that at least a portion of myth is the unconscious self-representation of the development of consciousness. We ought also to understand — and here analysts should be completely honest — that as matters now stand the patient "knows" his inner mechanisms the way a child learns his mother tongue. He cannot therefore defend himself nor exercise a critical spirit. I believe that this should make us hesitant and doubtful in the practice of therapy.

But to get back to Arion. The most useful instrument for an opening dialogue with the inner dimension of the person one is facing continues to be the dream, which stands apart from all rational judgment and can thus express psychological truths about the dreamer better than the dreamer himself can do consciously. Pascoli was quite right to say that "the dream is the infinite shadow of the True,"[7] as was Hugo that "we would judge men far more surely by their dreams than by their thoughts."[8]

Here then is our first reference to dreams. The patient, a painter who lives in the world of images and sensation, undergoes a prodigious flowering of dreams, which we will examine only partially, choosing the ones I consider most useful and significant for our purposes. Here is the first dream Arion brings:

> I am in a kind of limbo, with a very young girl on my left and my wife on my right. An old woman with claws appears; she assaults me and we fight. Defending myself, I understand that it is precisely these claws that make me suffer. I run away to escape these figures and find myself in a strange place, a sort of labyrinth made up of pits or caves, into which I will have to go at the risk of losing myself. In any case, I feel the need to see these places and then get away from them as quickly as possible.

In listening to a dream of this kind, one does not dwell on its details, for that would be to miss the forest for the trees. Every word of the dream refers to our culture, which is already familiar with this type of situation and can recall for us the solutions that have been provided for it in the course of our history. When the dreamer tells me that he finds himself "in a kind of limbo," if I know certain things — if I have the proper instrument — I can catch the meaning of this image with greater precision than someone without this knowledge. What can a limbo be? This word immediately projects us into that timeless dimension — present in all the great cosmogonic myths — in which everything is still understood in a fantastic totality that we may call, in Erich Neumann's word, "uroboric."[9] *Uroboros* is a Greek word that refers to the Egyptian alchemical figure of the serpent biting its tail: it is a perfect circle, enclosed in itself and self-sufficient. Its circular movement is paradoxically the expression of immobility and passivity, but at the same time the portent of an imminent creation.[10]

The patient, then, is telling me by this image that a process has been activated that expresses itself in the language of myth and which we must know how to read and interpret. This myth has to be able to penetrate into us so as to set in motion other images and thus activate that psychological and mythological process whereby man's developing consciousness leads him to his authentic existential condition.

At the beginning of the analytic relationship, Arion, although a culturally developed adult, is completely out of touch with his inner psychic dimension; in relation to that dimension he is thus immersed in a situation of nondifferentiation (the limbo), which goes back to a corresponding stage of humanity to which those myths expressing a complete union of man with nature refer. It is the situation in which man participates wholly in life, without ever questioning himself, since an ego, a consciousness capable of such questioning, does not yet exist. It is an existence devoid of conflicts and contradictions, corresponding probably to the intrauterine condition before birth. The lost paradise to which we sometimes look back with nostalgia is related precisely to this psychological experience that we have all lived through.

But the object of this nostalgia is illusory since, as we have known for some time, the world goes forward through conflict and differentiation. And indeed, in the dream we have just recorded, the patient, though perhaps suffering to the utmost, brings me the possibility of conflict: on one side there is a young woman, who expresses the new; on the other is his wife, with whom the dreamer has problems, as we will see later. He finds himself caught between these two dimensions, and then suffers an attack by an old woman with claws. It is this very image that, by its unreal, abnormal character, primarily attracts our attention. But if the dream has had the need to show a woman with claws, this means that some figure of this kind exists as symbolic reality in the dreamer himself; which is to say that on the psychological level he lives a relationship of fear with his own unconscious, expressed by this female figure.

In all mythologies we find the devouring Great Mother, for whom the development of the son signifies her own death. It is an archetypal model that is inevitably revealed every time the son (the ego) tries to break away from the suffocating hold of the mother (the unconscious) in order to begin a conscious and individual life. This destructive assault, which can be truly such if the ego is too weak to face it, also has an enormous motivational importance: the fear it arouses constitutes a ''transpersonal incentive'' to the development of consciousness.[11]

And indeed the dreamer is forced to act: he flees and finds himself before an opening of caves and abysses, into which he must penetrate and then emerge. In northern Spain there are prehistoric caves that one can approach only by crawling on all fours through artificially dug tunnels: it is surely a question of a ritual passage undertaken in order to reach a large room that receives light from above. To escape the limbo and the claws of the old woman, Arion must therefore perform an initiatory rite; he must enter again into the earth, dig, and see what is underneath, if he is to have the hope of entering a room where there is sunlight, the light that comes from above, the illumination of consciousness. It is a dream that, as often happens at the beginning of analysis, seems to sum up the whole psychic situation of the patient, and in a certain sense to indicate symbolically the path to follow.

I am sitting before him and receiving these messages in which I recognize a symbolic language. Should I communicate to the patient the deeper implications of his dream images? Of course, the presence of a suffering person raises questions of tact and technical ability, which cannot be separated from careful observation and an evaluation of his real capacity for understanding. We know that every time the ego — represented by the person of the dreamer himself — encounters figures of the unconscious — here personified by the wife, the young woman and the witch —new problems appear. Oddly enough, analysis does not resolve problems, but makes new ones emerge. It may seem incredible, but on the other hand it is childish to think that confronting the unconscious means finding solutions; generally a new set of problems is opened up, and we can never be sure that the person is capable of facing them. Hence the necessity of being very careful and of understanding what to communicate and what not to.

Consider then that every rent in the patient's psychic life does not lead to well-being, does not remove burdens from shoulders that are already weary, but adds new ones, which nevertheless illuminate the path to be taken and make it easier to follow. Confucius has said that we have a lamp on our backs that illuminates the past, but analysis makes it possible to put this lamp on our chests, and thus every patient who has undergone a successful analysis can say, like Tutankhamun: "I have seen yesterday; I know tomorrow.[12]

So then what do we see together? We see this person's attempt to emerge from a uroboric situation. All myths begin this way, that is, with the individual still enveloped in a gelatinous mass that protects him from the outside and from knowledge of himself. By asking for help, Arion is asking to be freed from this confused mass; but his request will lead to great suffering, since it involves the withdrawal of outside projections, which means giving up the idea that others are to blame for his discomfort and accepting the fact of being unconsciously guided in the formation of his destiny by internal transpersonal factors. It means realizing that one is no longer able to direct one's own consciousness, insofar as it is driven by those internal forces or structures that Jung calls archetypes.

In order for the patient to understand this, I must demonstrate to him how much of ancient man there is in him still, and I do not mean his personal historical past. It is certainly more reassuring to speak in personalistic terms and trace our discomfort back to our real mother or to our childhood relationships, but this would only partly be true. We must have the courage to state that just as our hearts are the same as that of any man of a hundred thousand years ago, so our psyches have been shaped for millennia to follow a certain mode of development. In each of us lies a profound area that is not subject to external conditionings and regulates our development apart from the environment. It is an inner "freedom" that operates autonomously; the archetypal structures inform our psychological dimension, exactly as the various cells are already prepared to follow their own development at the moment of conception. This is a notion that we might call entelechial in the sense that the psychic structure, like the biological one, "has in itself its own end," that is, a guiding principle that leads to the realization of all its potentialities.[13]

I consider it a great conquest for man to understand that he is not totally conditioned from the outside, as certain American psychologists would have it. I personally prefer to believe in an intrinsic possibility of defending ourselves against what we do not like, and I reject any explanation that denies our individual freedom. The conquest of that freedom passes through the always painful grasp of consciousness of what determines us *from inside*. It will therefore be necessary to allow the patient to transform into personal destiny, subjectively lived, the myth expressed through his dreams, associations and fantasy. Hercules who undergoes trials to gain immortality, Psyche who experiences countless mishaps in the search for her lost love — these myths should become, through the analysis, a personal destiny, something that moves us from within ourselves and allows us to achieve by our own strengths, and without imputing to anyone else the reasons for our suffering, that boon we call consciousness.

We know besides that for anyone who is summoned to this conquest there is no choice. Nor is it even clear that in terms of survival the search for consciousness is the best thing. Unamuno noted that "man, by the very fact of being man, of possessing consciousness, is, in comparison with the ass or the crab, a diseased animal. Consciousness is a disease."[14]

Arion's existence is thus marked by an apparent success to which a substantial defeat stands in opposition. The latter does not refer only to the present symptom that has brought him into analysis — that is, the fact that he finds it impossible to go on painting — but to something deeper of which the symptom is only an indication. Actually his real failure consists in being profoundly in discord with himself and in not being able to express his more genuine poetic intuition. The very success he finds on the outside is a mirror of this situation in that it implies the observance, albeit unconscious, of collective rules and standards, and thereby the betrayal of his own individual dimension. His creative block, the actual paralysis in which the patient finds himself, makes the conflict and the split between what he is in appearance and what he still obscurely feels himself to be inside all too perceptible. We might even speak of a schizophrenic episode, if this term, beyond its etymological meaning, did not have an exclusively pathological connotation. It is in any case an "extreme situation," to use a term from existential philosophy, in which one experiences an uneasiness that goes far beyond any specific ordinary symptoms, which indeed are often completely absent.

It is interesting to note that when we find ourselves in such a state of disorientation, it is not easy for us to get out of it by ourselves, and it is also possible that religious themes may emerge. This gives rise to the need for communion, forgiveness, liberation and atonement. In these cases a medical response is of no use; when a person is experiencing this condition there are two possible responses: the religious one, which is not within the analyst's sphere, and the psychological one, which invites the person to look at himself, to know himself, to compare what he is with what he might be. This is by no means an easy task. We can all make the experiment of pausing a moment, ignoring all external stimulations and trying to look ourselves in the face: we will realize how difficult and painful it all is and how much it is tied to a sense of oppression that comes from outside. It is as though we had opened a peephole on reality. Sometimes we are frightened by it to the point of wishing for death. Kafka has given a good description of this experience: "A first sign of nascent knowledge is the desire for death. This life seems unendurable, any other unattainable."[15]

Fortunately, however, neurotic torment is often so intense that we are driven to overcome this difficulty; from this arises the appeal for help. But in order to understand another's suffering and be able to offer him help, it is necessary to set in motion that type of empathic attitude whereby the message sent to us takes on relevance for our own lives. And perhaps the more remote from us this message seems, the more that person may have been sent by "destiny" in order that we the analysts, faced with his questions, may put questions to ourselves. In such a case, it is highly useful to observe our dreams, side by side with the patient's, and our associations, since it is very probable that the presence of his problem may trigger in us some response or knowledge.

We have seen the dream in which the patient finds himself in a kind of limbo with three women, and must start digging in order to make his way into certain caves. We have said that this dream presents us at the beginning with a protective uroboric situation, by now illusory, from which it is necessary to escape since it has no history and no life. These first communications trigger in the other an emotional response that in the sphere of the analysis is expressed through dreams. After the first session, Arion brings me this dream:

> I see a blue sky, with a kind of large zodiac; it is like a luminous sphere or a flying saucer. Then I go down into some excavations where there are mummies, one definitely of a woman with her legs apart, and a statue that looks like a female Jupiter. There are holes; I am frightened, but know I must fill them as quickly as possible.

In his presence I preserve a receptive and attentive attitude, knowing that I cannot and must not reduce his existence simply to his personal past. I also know that I must supply him with the tools whereby to understand how his psychological situation of the moment is in a certain sense the actualization of a very ancient myth. Indeed, we see in the dream a great juxtaposition of light and darkness, represented by the sky and the excavations. The light and darkness immediately remind us of the origin of life: there is no myth or popular tradition that has not depicted the creation of the world as a separation of sky and earth, of light from darkness, as for example in the Maori myth of creation.[16] In Egyptian mythology, the first creative act is an egg born of the river, from which emerges Ra, the sun god. Genesis too, to whose cultural matrix we all belong, is nothing but the exemplification of the birth of light from darkness; while for Heraclitus, the sun is born anew each day. These are things that I know, and I also feel I have experienced them through my own analysis; I truly believe in them, and the patient perceives the love that is present in my response.

But what are we doing at this moment from a theoretical standpoint? Like all of us, the patient belongs to a culture that has made the world what it is; he has behind him a scientific tradition that claims to have discovered the immutable laws of a world in which identity and uniformity operate, and before which we are virtually crushed. This is to say that we are brought up to take an objective view of things and recognize in them an intrinsic reality of their own. Everything that has preceded us offers itself to us as a real, concrete, immutable fact. Our "this can be done" or "this can't be done" are related to the inner law that Freud was to call the superego, and to the external laws that govern us and indicate to us the path to follow regardless of our own reality. Coming into the world, we find everything already made, and when we collide with external reality — that is, when our awareness is awakened in childhood and finds a dimension of life already completely structured—we have the impression that it is also immutable. Hence the necessity, and at the same time the difficulty, of grasping the essence of mythical communication, which also belongs to our human dimension.

But why should science, or reason in general, combat myth? Probably it has sound reasons. When Newton, for example, conceives of universal gravity, he must do battle with the mythical idea that the planets are moved by an inner vital force. Science as such *must* do battle, because at the root of the myth lies what is called "perception of expression," while in scientific conceptions what counts is the immutability of laws. [17]

This is what allows the scientist to establish the exact path of a spaceship: the law of gravity is the same everywhere, as are the equations capable of governing a flight. But in the presence of a suffering person what words can be of help? The law of gravity is no longer of any use, since human reality does not possess that objectivity that science claims for its subject. This is not to deny the importance of the scientific approach, but to recognize its limitations. The words that make it possible for us to save someone's life do not result from "objective" knowledge but from the "perception of expression." This formula implies the existence, over and above the concrete and factual world, of a subjective reality that inevitably colors our vision. In this sense a rigorously determined objective world is a pure abstraction, and we find ourselves living instead in a world that can assume different aspects in relation to our emotional state. "In love and hate, in hope and fear, in joy and terror the features of reality are transformed," [18] as we all surely know. There does not exist therefore for human experience a single, unmistakable and already given reality, but only emotional states that cause us to experience the external world in a fluctuating manner. This is the root of myth.

During the analytic process it is necessary to release the person from rigorous certainties, which, among other things, serve only to crush him, in order to transport him, by our faith in what we communicate, into the reality of the mythical world, as determined by his own emotion. This is the fundamental step: to get the patient to understand how his emotion and feelings portray the world in which he finds himself. For example, many disturbances of a sexual nature derive no benefit from the most advanced medical treatment since the root of the problem lies on the emotional plane. On the other hand, it is possible that everything may dissolve like snow in the sun when the person understands that the genesis of his illness does not reside in a malfunctioning cell or organ, but in the emotional dimension that hinders his inner communication.

To make a person understand the perception of expression means to encourage him to perceive the way in which he expresses himself in the sphere of his own emotionality. Then it is possible to see how the patient slowly relives a former psychological climate, which recalls the mythical moments of the birth of the world, with the appearance of light out of darkness.

In Arion's second dream, a kind of female Jupiter appears, and a goddess with "legs apart." This last detail, coupled with the previous dream, shows how the female element presents itself on the psychological plane in a twofold manner: as a mother who gives birth but at the same time is prepared to welcome her own fruit back into herself, to reconstitute that original "limbo" from which the patient instead must emerge by facing up to himself. This is the situation revealed by his first contact with the inner dimension — descending into the excavations — and at this point he is seized with fear.

But what is this feeling? There is nobody on earth who does not know it, and even the most seemingly secure person has his well-hidden fears. In this case, the fear indicates that the patient is beginning to perceive the power of the uroboric situation that envelops him and prevents him from moving toward differentiation, offering in exchange a security that he only gives up with great difficulty. Even the child, at the moment when the ego emerges and must detach itself from the figure of the mother, experiences this feeling of anxiety, similar to the one we all undergo as adults when we pass from a situation of presumed security to a new and as yet unknown one. In other words, every forward step taken to free ourselves from whatever is holding us back is marked by fear. Everything that does not belong to the past and does not form part of our introjected experience necessarily presents itself as something threatening, because we have no ready categories by which to recognize what is happening. These categories are provided by the group, and thus every time we are afraid it may be that we are trying to do something individual. Where instead fear is absent, we are unconsciously submerged in the group and in the teachings of the past.

This discourse is valid at any level and implies the continuous dialectic between individual and group, a dialectic in which we all move, and which, as we will see, will allow Arion to emerge from his suffering.

Let us now try to describe more clearly the psychological situation of the patient at the moment in which he is seized by panic. Once again the knowledge of man's myths and cultural history makes it possible to give his personal anxiety a much broader scope. What he fears is paradoxically the very goal he is seeking, namely separation, differentiation, emergence from the "earthly paradise." But this does not reflect only a personal resistance on his part to psychological growth, at least at that moment, but also the general "inertia of the psyche," which, as Erich Neumann points out, "cannot be called a desire to remain unconscious; on the contrary, *that* is the natural thing."[19] In other words, our natural condition is unconsciousness and

the ascent toward consciousness is the 'unnatural' thing in nature; it is specific of the species Man. . . . The struggle between the specifically human and the universally natural constitutes the history of man's conscious development.[20]

Thus, contrary to what one may think, our conscious existence is not something natural, but an actual conquest that cannot be accomplished without fear and sacrifice. Adam and Eve would never have left the earthly paradise without the temptation of the devil, that is, without the intervention of an antagonistic will opposed to remaining permanently in the uroboric situation, in which man, writes Neumann, "drowses in the unconscious, contained in the infinite like a fish in the environing sea."[21]

The patient's fear is therefore the "physiological" and necessary reaction that enables him to take a first step toward becoming aware of his own individual identity, and it gives us in some way a confirmation of his "wish," albeit unconscious, to proceed on this path.

2

Solitude and Psychology

In the dreams of Arion we have examined so far, and in others belonging to the same period, we find female images endowed with considerable power. Pursuing our parallel between the individual's psychological development and the development of humanity as expressed in myths, we may advance the hypothesis that the patient is living on the personal plane an experience that has already occurred — whether historically or only psychologically doesn't matter — in the evolution of humanity. I refer to what Bachofen calls the "matriarchal age," [22] without, however, taking this to stand for a definite moment in history, but rather a psychic structural dimension that can also be reflected on the sociological plane, whether or not power is actually held by women.

According to Bachofen, the matriarchal group is characterized by a particular spirit of intimacy, by a type of communication absolutely lacking in cultural and educational superstructures. It is a group wherein the emotional relationship between a mother and her children predominates, and it implies the existence of strong inner ties. We could speak once more of the total undifferentiation of the individual to which we referred in connection with the "limbo"; as Neumann writes, "Bachofen's matriarchate stands for the stage when ego consciousness is undeveloped and still embedded in nature and the world." [23]

It is thus a paradisiacal condition in which existence is fully enjoyed in its immediacy, at an unconscious and vegetative level. The laws governing the course of existence are the purely natural and instinctual ones, which with regularity and without tensions flow along with the rhythms of birth, growth and death. This probably corresponds to a certain conception of happiness, linked to a lack of conflicts and guilt feelings. And it is perhaps this idea of happiness that prompted Camus to remark that the only thing more tragic than suffering is the life of a happy man. [24]

A further characteristic of this typically maternal (in the transpersonal sense) constellation is its immutability. Nature, indeed, is always identical to itself, and the law of instinct, in Neumann's words, "subserves the propagation, preservation, and evolution of the species rather than the development of the single individual."[25]

From this standpoint, the generous and protective mother, who nourishes and defends her children, becomes the devouring mother — recall the old woman with claws in Arion's first dream — who does everything in her power to hamper the development of the son from the moment he tries to escape the circle of her influence.

It may simply be a reflection of one of our cultural prejudices, but I do think that a society based on the biological unity of mother and children, which is satisfied with a protective happiness, cannot be progressive. The evolution of culture requires individual intervention to break the uniformity of the course of nature and divert it toward different goals. This causes deep feelings of guilt, conflicts and responsibilities: a new law emerges, one we might call superego, which recalls each individual to his or her human and social duties. I do not mean to pronounce value judgments, but I simply note how the rigid superego, characteristic of patriarchal societies, is the spring that impels people to greater achievements. We might indeed advance the hypothesis that the achievement is actually a way of confronting, and to a certain extent overcoming, a sense of guilt for having produced a gap in the continuity of nature.

One of the consequences of development in the patriarchal direction is the appearance at the social level of the dimension of power, which, according to Bachofen, would seem to be absent in organizations of the matriarchal kind. But negative as this aspect may be, we must recognize that the absolute protection offered by matriarchal society, intrinsically based on dependence and on the most elementary needs, is much more oppressive than a situation in which domination can be opposed by a contrary will operating by action and ideas. In this dialectic between freedom and dependence, we can immediately identify one of the crucial points characterizing our existence, and we might say that any important choice we make implies this polarity. I stress again that the choice of freedom inevitably evokes guilt feelings, but we cannot take a single step forward if we do not cut those ties that simultaneously mean security and dependence. It is certainly not a question of accomplishing such an act once and for all, since life confronts us daily with choices. Nor do I believe that a person can always live in freedom, but I am convinced that any existence that is truly such must be marked by this tendency toward freedom.

But what is it that gives us the strength to be free and to make this choice, which deprives us of all security that does not come from within ourselves? I believe it to be a deep sense of self-esteem. And with this, let us return to the problem of the patient: a person who, even though he has gained the recognition of the world outside, preserves within himself a negative image and does not believe in what he is doing. From a certain standpoint, his indifference in the face of other people's esteem represents an advantage in that these external signs of approval no longer have the capacity to strengthen him. Let us repeat that the strength and security of our actions come from ourselves and solely from ourselves. As Rilke wrote to the young poet Kappus: "You are looking outward, and that above all you should not do now. Nobody can counsel and help you, nobody. There is only one single way. Go into yourself."[26]

My job as an analyst is to see that Arion recovers his self-esteem. But in such cases words are not enough, since on the psychological plane nonverbal communication is much more important, and this always takes place within the analytic relationship. It is my own existence and personal self-esteem that will nourish the patient. Once again this requires that I examine myself and question my own security and my faith in what I am doing. The patient's wounds make it necessary for the analyst to reopen his own, and to re-establish contact with that deep dimension in which self-esteem is rooted.

The human condition, unlike that of other animal species, is marked by a very long period of dependence on the parents. The child's survival is concretely tied to the nourishment supplied by the mother. But from the earliest phases of existence, and precisely because of the child's psychophysical immaturity, a kind of psychological nourishment, which should likewise come from the mother, is no less important. It is in these very early moments that the basis for future self-esteem is laid, even though we are not yet able to formulate precisely what the mother's correct attitude in relation to the child—one capable of generating in him a positive image of himself—should be. We can say, however, that in general the child's early experience in his relationship with the mother is articulated in three fundamental and closely interconnected dimensions: his own body, the outside world (human or not) and his self-image from a psychological standpoint. In this uroboric phase of the child's total identity with the mother who satisfies his needs, writes Neumann,

to be fed, warmed, and sheltered is to be blissfully taken care of by
the world, the "other," and "oneself." In this sense the primary relation is the ontogenetic foundation for being "in the world," "with an
other," "by oneself." . . .

Future health and success in life depend in great measure upon the
development during early childhood of these three originally still in-
dissoluble relationships. [27]

By taking care to satisfy the child's primary needs, the mother makes
up for the inevitable frustrations that life brings from its very first
moments, and thus generates a feeling of security and trust that allows

the formation of a positively integrated ego, that is, one able to assimilate and integrate even negative qualities, whether disagreeable facts
in the outer world or inner factors such as cravings, pain, and so on. [28]

If the mother lacks a profound attitude of acceptance and does not
succeed in carrying out this basic compensatory function, the conditions can be laid for a psychological disturbance linked to the absence of that "affirmative feeling toward one's own personality"[29]
that we call self-esteem. In this case, the next transition indispensable to the individual's psychological development — that is, relin-
quishing the mother's protection — does not take place or becomes
extremely difficult. The ego, in fact, is not prepared to undergo the
inevitable and completely normal conflict that arises at a certain
moment between the permanence of the primary relation and the
automorphic tendency to individual development. The working hypothesis to which the concept of *automorphism* refers involves the
existence of a mechanism of internal regulation by which, at the moment when the paradisiacal state of total protection becomes an obstacle
to the further growth of the child, feelings of hatred and aggression
spontaneously arise to facilitate detachment from the mother figure.

Even in our adult lives we may sometimes find ourselves in relationships that have already said everything they have to say and are
now suffocating to us; only by experiencing hatred and aggression
are we able to get out of them. It is as though we are seized by inner
forces that drive us to a dialectical confrontation with bonds that have
become unreal.

Normal psychological development thus passes through a primary
relation in which we are completely involved and which allows us to
structure the kind of inner security and self-esteem that later gains
substance in the possibility of undergoing the conflict between the

emerging ego, which is becoming aware of itself, and the undifferentiated primary situation. In other words, it is possible to enter into a dialectical relationship with another — with the mother, in the case of the developing child — only if one is ready to accept the coexistence of good and evil, and to tolerate the feeling of guilt that assails us every time we cut our ties with the past.

Jean Rostand has said that "to be adult is to be alone."[30] The truth of this statement, suggested perhaps by his biological experiments, has a psychological basis. When suprapersonal factors impel the child to separate from the mother, in reality structural changes have already taken place whereby the protection offered by the mother has been introjected, and this inner security guides the child's actions even in the real mother's absence. According to Neumann:

> The lack of agreement between the personal reality of the parents and the child's psychic apperception of it is very striking and is one of the central problems of child psychology. Psychic development seems to be archetypally directed from inside, and when, for example, the time has come for a child — genetically speaking — to sever its ties with the mother and the maternal world, the mother will appear a "witch" quite independently of her "real" behavior. For the sake of the child's development all the actual facts of the situation are now, necessarily and meaningfully, worked out in accordance with the "witch" idea. If the mother is really "wicked," then to all intents and purposes she *is* a witch; if she is "good," she is a witch just the same, whose very goodness beguiles her offspring into remaining childish.[31]

The transition to adulthood thus takes place in an atmosphere of love and struggle: struggle, since we must free ourselves in any case; love, since within ourselves we carry the ineradicable traces of the warmest moments of our lives, like a flower hidden in grass and of which we can only smell the aroma.

Freud was of the opinion that a certain partiality on the part of the mother, an excess of love lavished on the child, laid the foundations for the latter's future success:

> I have found that people who know that they are preferred or favoured by their mother give evidence in their lives of a peculiar self-reliance and an unshakeable optimism which often seem like heroic attributes and bring actual success to their possessors.[32]

The problem of solitude and of being an adult should then be placed within the framework of an inner strength that draws only on itself and can do without the short-lived shadows of the outside world. To emerge from protection, or from the wish for protection, is thus one of man's tasks, even at the risk of suffering.

The myth of an earthly paradise very clearly expresses how history had its beginning at the moment when man, driven by a demoniacal impulse, picked the fruit of good and evil. The myth, however, becomes a real and living experience when a person, in his life or in the analytic process, comes face to face with his or her own personal problem. And it is in the language of his very dreams that I am able to give the patient the information he needs if he is to understand himself.

Here then is Arion in another dream:

> I find myself in an uncomfortable and dangerous situation; suddenly I see coming toward me a vague, amoeboid, gelatinous mass. Examining it carefully, I realize that it is taking on my appearance. I then begin to speak in German to this other self because I know that this is the language used in circuses to tame wild beasts.

In order to decipher a still unknown script, it is necessary to have a knowledge of the subject, and this is true here as well — that is, to understand the language in which the patient's unconscious expresses itself, we need reference points that will allow us to see a psychological meaning in the dream message. Here the reason for the ''double'' or second self — which often appears in literature, ethnology and the history of religions, as Otto Rank has shown in detail[33] — emerges with sufficient clarity. We know that the central theme in many stories is the dramatic encounter with an image of oneself,[34] an alter ego that compels us to a confrontation or an irreparable break. This occurs, for example, with the doubling of personality illustrated in the novels of Robert Louis Stevenson.

Knowledge of mythology and literature allows both me and the patient to understand, at least in part, the meaning of the double, by connecting our particular experience with more general but analogous situations on the psychological plane. One of the possible explanations, which is also the most widespread, sees the ''other'' who is juxtaposed to the subject as the expression of a different modality of existence emerging from a profound need within the subject himself. But the myth also warns us that the sight of one's own image is always connected with the fear of death.[35] What we actually fear is the loss of our personality, of the identity in which we recognize ourselves, threatened by the confrontation with unknown aspects of ourselves that question our whole existence. This is the most dramatic meaning of psychosis, because in it not only does the confrontation with darkness, the negative other, take place, but the darkness itself submerges the ego. It is for this very reason that madness frightens us, and the great journeys into madness are often, as in the cases of Nietzsche and Hölderlin, journeys of no return. Jung, too, experienced something of the kind, but according to his own testimony it had been a desired and anticipated psychosis. He was, however, of the opinion that "the difference is not always clearly perceived and this gives rise to uncertainty or even a fit of panic."[36]

Arion thus finds himself face to face with an unclear element of his personality, one that indeed has not yet assumed a definite form — it is a "gelatinous mass" — and he finds it so dangerous that he associates it with a ferocious beast that must be tamed by speaking German. This is a language that in reality he does not know, just as the unconscious is unknown to his conscious attitude. But through analysis he can learn to speak this new language, which will allow him to make contact with the amoeboid form that frightens him so much. We will have to make a patient effort to mold this psychological dimension, which at present sets itself against the ego and continues to escape understanding, but even by its protean nature expresses plasticity and the possibility of transformation.

We can say that the analysis of this patient has been shot through with fear from the beginning, and in many of his dreams there are difficult situations that he overcomes, without however losing his feeling of uncertainty and dread. This is a fact that I, as the analyst, must take into account, since it gives me a clinical indication of the progress of the analysis. The fear raised by the encounter with unconscious processes warns me, in fact, of the gravity of the situation, that is, of the depth of the dynamics being set in motion and of the risks involved. I have said before that fear, just like love, has an enormous cognitive importance. Indeed, fear and Eros are closely connected,[37] and it is easy enough to observe in our experience how it is precisely situations of love and panic, with their intense emotional charge, that cause completely new and unknown aspects of our personality to emerge.

This does not, however, keep fear from also expressing the particular harshness of the collision between consciousness and the unconscious, characteristic not only of the patient, but of all of us who are personally experiencing one of the most important phenomena of Western culture: in addition to its meaning in the therapeutic sphere, psychoanalysis as a vision of the world implies the relative status of the ego, which is dethroned from its central position in the personality and forced into a painful confrontation with other, no less important forces. As Thomas Mann observed:

> And is man's ego a thing imprisoned in itself and sternly shut up in its boundaries of flesh and time? Do not many of the elements which make it up belong to a world before it and outside of it? The notion that each person is himself and can be no other, is that anything more than a convention, which arbitrarily leaves out of account all the transitions which bind the individual consciousness to the general?[38]

The situation is analogous to the one that man formerly experienced when he learned that the earth is not the center of the universe. Freud himself, in an essay written in 1917, states that psychoanalysis constitutes a psychological revolution equivalent to the Copernican one, since

> the psychological research of the present time . . . seeks to prove to the ego that it is not even master in its own house, but must content itself with scanty information of what is going on unconsciously in its mind.[39]

This dethroning of the ego, which occurs through the emergence of other forces normally held at bay by defense mechanisms, cannot help but arouse fears and uncertainties. This is because we are placed in a situation that goes beyond the sphere of "reason" and are no longer capable of mastering it with the instruments of the ego. Why, for example, is the child afraid of the dark? Because, in the temporary absence of a known and concretely perceptible reality, he fills that void with himself, that is, with his own unconscious. Or, why do we all to a certain degree fear unknown places? Precisely because we do not find anything that can be related to our experience and our usual categories are no longer of any use to us. What emerges is therefore a new and unknown dimension, which must be accepted as real since the fear we feel in its presence is real. Thus from the moment in which the patient asks for my help because he is experiencing suffering that cannot be explained in rational terms, a suffering that stands apart from all apparent success and external achievement, he finds himself necessarily reckoning with a psychic world that ousts the ego from its dominant position and lowers it into what Jung calls "a dark state of disorientation."[40]

The as yet indistinct appearance of the "other self" that figures in the dream essentially expresses the difficulty of defining, by the categories of the ego and in terms of any reality known to us, an equally concrete, albeit elusive reality, the one that Jung calls the "reality of the soul." Arion, in this phase, is thus experiencing a profound schism within himself, as is also suggested by the theme of the double. Writes Jung:

> This collapse and disorientation of consciousness may last a consider-able time and it is one of the most difficult transitions the analyst has to deal with. . . . It is a sign that the patient is being driven along willy-nilly without any sense of direction . . . in an utterly *soulless* condition, exposed to the full force of autoerotic affects and fantasies.[41]

Indeed, a twofold risk exists from the moment when the ego loses control of psychic life and its conviction of being able to dominate the world with the light of reason. The fear of psychic breakdown, aroused by the encounter with the unconscious, can be such as to paralyze completely the ongoing psychological process, and thereby to reinforce the usual attitude of the conscious ego, which rediscovers in its own rigidity a support and an apparent strength by which to counter the irruptions of the unconscious. In cases of this kind, the patient may also break off the analysis and try to overcome his difficulties in other ways experienced as less dangerous.

The second risk is that consciousness is not strong enough and founders in the unconscious, succumbing to the attraction that the latter in any case exercises. This is the "loss of soul" so feared by primitives,[42] the dissolution of the ego in the primal matrix, the annihilation of self in what Neumann calls "uroboric incest."[43] In such cases, the analyst must carry out an operation of containment, supplying the patient with the orientation and protection that he needs.[44]

Between these two extremes there exists a third possibility, that is, that the individual, faced with the upsurge of the irrational, and though feeling profoundly his own disorientation and the fear of losing himself, will be able to go through this split and inner conflict by agreeing to question the categories with which he customarily looks at the world. This may involve enormous depression, disorientation and uncertainty, but it also implies an elasticity and plasticity of the ego that constitute the true condition for any further development. Indeed, contrary to common opinion, the truly strong man is not the one who excludes the irrational and emotional element from his life, adopting a rigid, narrow-minded and one-sided attitude, but the one who is also capable of including in the categories of reality inconsistency and doubt, and therefore the possibility of change.

In other words, it is not a question of fleeing before the irrational but of stopping to look at it, confident, like Seneca, that "there is nothing too difficult and arduous for the mind of man to be able to master and that does not become familiar by constant meditation."[45]

Perhaps at this point it is necessary to make a distinction. It is absolutely true that the psychic field is an accumulation of experiences and feelings that are difficult to classify, just as it is true that the irrational element takes up the lion's share of the sphere of unconscious processes. But there is also the rather important moment of intersubjective communication, which has very precise rules. I cannot communicate by the same language as the unconscious, since communication to be such must not be contradictory. Now, although convinced, as Jung says, that "every unequivocal, so-called 'clear' answer always remains stuck in the head and seldom penetrates to the heart,"[46] we cannot forget that one must also make an effort to make intelligible what at first is confused. And intersubjective communication can also exist between my ego and the unconscious. If the latter remains confused, as it is by definition, it will never be salutary for my consciousness.

My effort as a therapist will therefore be to translate together with the patient, reasonably and as faithfully as possible, the irrational aspects of his life.

3

The Development of Consciousness

We have spoken of the primary relation with the mother, and of its fundamental importance for the individual's psychological development. We have also said that at a certain point the child succeeds in detaching himself from it, thanks to an aggressive attitude toward the mother, an attitude that arises spontaneously as soon as he perceives that he is different and separate. In the case of the woman, differentiation occurs with greater difficulty and the period of time spent in uroboric identity is much longer, with consequences on the psychological plane that are reflected in a different way of confronting existence.

In this connection, I am thinking of an excellent film, *The Lacemaker*, which underscores the difference and importance of the woman's psychic world in relation to the man's. It is a very subtle work and shows how certain feminine values, profoundly true ones, are systematically crushed. Feminine feeling, as a psychological function that can and should prevail, is set against a masculine narrow-mindedness that while not neurotic is absolutely incapable of feeling. And the film's message is aimed at the extensive recovery of feminine values, even on the part of the man, who must learn that feeling and love are more important than power. This is an illuminating recognition for the psychological development of a person, whether man or woman. Much has been said, and is still being said, about the oppressed condition of women, but one ought to understand that men too are victims, insofar as they are exclusively engaged in the struggle for power. We might say that they are victims of their own prejudices, which have transformed some indispensable components of their existence into negative values. Hence the necessity of acknowledging these components and showing the illusory and negative nature of such values as power, which separate man from himself and from harmonious relations with other men — though it is useful to remember Melville's cautionary words:

> For be a man's intellectual superiority what it will, it can never assume the practical, available supremacy over other men, without the aid of some sort of external arts and entrenchments, always, in themselves, more or less paltry and base.[47]

The woman's longer attachment within the maternal uroboros means that she will seek in life what has nourished her for such a length of time, and this is perhaps the reason why she tends to experience relationships with greater intensity. While knowledge and objectivity are of prime importance to the man, the woman has to be able to love. The reality, however, is that men are for the most part extremely superficial in their feelings. Let us try to understand why.

We can advance the hypothesis that the male child in the sphere of the primary relation already feels his own diversity from the mother, and it is very likely that she too stimulates him in this direction. He is therefore in a greater hurry to emerge from the maternal world, to distance himself from it, even with violence, in order to make his way to the patriarchal world. The time he spends within a fundamental relationship such as the one with his mother is much shorter, and this imprinting helps to make the adult man virtually incapable of true relationships. Like Odysseus, he never commits himself, and must always move on because he cannot dwell in any situation. The essential difference in the first phases of development of the male and female child will set the man and woman on completely different paths, radicalizing and making concrete, through cultural and educational stereotypes as well, a profound gap between two modes of existence that are equally necessary and second nature to human beings of both sexes.

It is important, however, to understand that this rupture is the indispensable condition for the development of individual consciousness, which emerges precisely through conflict, that is, through the breakup of an undifferentiated totality — which we have called uroboric — into antithetical pairs of opposites that allow the ego to take a position on one or the other side, to make choices, and thus to give itself an orientation. This is what the myth expresses metaphorically by the "separation of the world parents,"[48] the differentiation of the father and mother, that is to say of the first great pair of opposites experienced by man.

But every polar opposition implies a dimension of evaluation and therefore goes back to the distinction between good and evil. During an analysis, it is always possible to see how, in the patient's hindsight, the father and mother alternately represent *good* and *bad*: it is one of the structural realities of existence to experience opposition in such a way that everything good is projected onto one of the terms and everything bad onto the other. This might explain, at least in part, the psychological significance of the introduction of a "third" into the

sphere of the couple, which allows the re-establishment of that tri-
adic structure wherein the child for the first time perceives the separation of the parents and the distinction between good and evil.

But this differentiation of opposites is always accompanied by a
sense of guilt because, as we have seen at the ontogenetic level and as
the myths confirm, this takes place by an aggressive act against the
original, omniscient and "divine" totality, which is shattered so that
it can be assimilated and known: the knowledge of good and evil is
truly our "original sin," the one that makes us men and women and
at the same time condemns us to a perennial conflict with ourselves.[49]

All this is particularly obvious every time we perform an act of
liberation, that is, whenever we make a qualitative leap in the sphere
of emotions, ideas or work. To change our reality requires sacrifice
and suffering, insofar as every liberation is always linked to a prohibition by the conservative superego. If we succeed, however, in tolerat-
ing our sense of guilt for having broken this unwritten but no less
potent law, we also succeed in grasping the creative value of our act
of separation and detachment from a past that immobilizes us.

This is what Arion, too, is going through in the analysis, and his
dreams continue to offer specific evidence of his psychological
experience. Here are two consecutive ones:

> I find myself pedaling a very high bicycle. I am afraid of losing con-
> trol of it and indeed do so at a certain point. The moment I am about to
> fall I succeed in regaining my balance but I regain it completely only
> when I arrive at my destination. I then have a quarrel with an old man;
> there is also a woman present, who in her turn argues with the old
> man. I defend her, take her away and kiss her on the mouth.

> I am in a public square, one familar to me, but now it is completely
> demolished. Someone shows me a deep well and urges me to descend
> into it. I start to lower myself, but there are no steps, only jutting
> rocks to which to hold. Seized by fear, I stop, look desperately up-
> ward and cry out that I can't do it.

These dreams reflect what we have been saying all along. In the
first one, the dreamer finds himself on a bicycle, a means of locomo-
tion that proceeds by virtue of his own strength. His fear of falling
can be seen, within the effort he is making to emancipate himself, as
the fear that what he is doing is wrong and also beyond his capabilities.
But just at the moment when he arrives at his destination he realizes
that he can do it. Thus, despite his fears, Arion succeeds in grasping

and accepting his own individuality, and this brings him to a certain goal. It has taken a real act of courage, and so he comes to meet an old man and a woman who are quarreling. He intervenes and separates them. When a male and a female figure appear in a dream, it is easy enough to recognize them as the parental couple, and the fact that the dreamer interposes himself between them probably shows his perception of something he should have carried out long ago but, for reasons that we do not know, did not — namely the separation of the parents.

The kiss, too, is a significant element: to kiss this woman on the mouth means no longer to consider the mother as such but as a woman. In general, dreams of incestuous acts are experienced with a good deal of anxiety, but one must understand how this seemingly scandalous situation can actually express, within the process of development, an act of liberation. Among the Hottentots, for example, the initiation of a boy into adult life provides for the son's ritual union with his mother, precisely because it is through the active possession of the mother herself that the necessary detachment from the child's world takes place. It is even possible to interpret psychologically as unconscious initiatory rites certain seductions within the family sphere.

The second dream is also part of the process. We have already said that in our existence it is not possible to take a step forward without having to pay a price, and in this case the perspective and impetus contained in the first dream are repaid by fear. To gain awareness means for the patient to come closer to confrontation with his own inner failure, and for this reason he must be afraid. At the moment when someone — in whom we may recognize the analyst — invites him to descend into the well, he realizes that things are not so easy as one might have thought and remains quite paralyzed with fear. In this circumstance, I must be very cautious, since I have no assurance that he will be able to come back out. The only support we have is the psychological field created in the analytic relationship: I am there with him, and even if he does not know it, he is not alone in his descent into the inferno. An intuitive perception on my part convinces me that the game is worth the candle, and therefore I accompany him in his descent, balancing his fear with my faith.

Dreams of this kind constitute very important messages for both analyst and patient, since they serve to inform us about the difficulties of the situation, or indeed about the kind of resistance that the patient's psychological constitution, which is the result of both his

personal history and elements that transcend the individual, offers to
the exploration of certain themes that emerge by the very fact of our
turning our attention to them. When people say that in order to practice psychotherapy it is unnecessary for the psychologist to have been
analyzed — as is required on the other hand for the exercise of psychoanalysis — they are actually talking nonsense since any therapeutic
relationship itself evokes and activates problems in both partners,
and if these problems are not faced up to with a certain knowledge
gained only through analysis they may do more harm than good.

What counts at these particular moments is inner resonance, that
is, the subliminal perception of events that allows us to guide the
situation. A classic example of this modality is to be seen in courtship,
where it is not words that are important but the deep feeling that
derives from the underground communication of mutual sentiments.
Thus, in the sphere of analysis, which has points of contact with love,
one acts in a particular way so that certain things will be understood
implicitly, because one has an intuitive perception of them — for
example, that the analysand may succeed or not. This is a kind of
sensitivity that develops with practice and needs continually to be
sharpened, but it also requires a natural gift for seizing on those nonverbal communications that occur in any psychological relationship.

We have seen that Arion is living at the level of his own personal
experience what in mythological terms is called the "separation of
the parents," or of opposites. We have also said that this is a structural reality of man, whose brain is adapted in such a way as to function only within a series of oppositions, reducible to the fundamental
male-female couple, and of which we find expressions in even the
oldest cultures. Chinese philosophy, for example, is based on the
Yang-Yin polarity, respectively the male and female principles. To
respond briefly to those who might say that such a juxtaposition is
now obsolete, let me point out that our discourse is purely psychological, and that a male reality and a female reality exist, whose
psychological significance we must understand, without concerning
ourselves with how they may be institutionalized. This last is simply
a question of power: if in patriarchal society masculine values pre-
dominate, in the matriarchal kind it is the feminine values that hold
sway.

At the moment during the development process when the mother-
father polarity is constellated, an immediate change takes place in
the emotional sphere. The original "wholeness" of the undifferenti-

ated condition is broken, and for the first time opposing feelings like love and hatred are perceived. Identification with a single one of the poles and the blurring or repression of the other are the next immediate step, which structures the consciousness of the ego and with it the fundamental split in our psyche. We then learn, for example, to experience love consciously and to repress the feeling of hatred into the unconscious. But if this split takes on excessive proportions and there is no longer any relation between the ego and the unconscious, it is possible at a certain point for the repressed aspects to take over and remove all power from the ego.

It is characteristic of the analytic process to bring to consciousness the fundamental problem of ambivalence. Although this term can be applied to a number of fields, the emotional one seems to be the chosen space where ambivalence reigns supreme. Love and hatred are omnipresent, and the awareness of this archaic and profound psychic dimension produces disorientation and incredulity. And yet the analytic experience and the wider and tragic field of life continually confirm the bitter truth of ambivalence. There is no love that is not also destruction. But this condition is so burdensome that people very often prefer to repress one of the poles.

The loss of the original wholeness — the identification of consciousness with a single pole of the conflict, and the blurring of the other — is experienced as a primary loss: what is irrevocably lost is the original sense of unity in which one is completely immersed and protected, like a child in the body of the mother. Birth, both at the biological level and at the psychological one, can thus be experienced as an emotional trauma or amputation. It is an experience that always recurs in our existence — for example, whenever the uroboric situation that we have unconsciously reconstituted in the relationship with a partner is broken. The pangs of love may seem hopeless, and this is because they re-evoke on the personal plane the great transpersonal adventure of man, who detaches himself from whatever is protective in order to enter into a new phase of existence. Our entire life is strewn with these moments of separation, and the suffering that this involves is never merely personal. Indeed, one is activating very deep psychic dynamics that go back to a transpersonal situation of man: the original union and its loss.

There are people with such a fear of separation that they never fall in love, never become involved in relationships of dependency. For psychological reasons, they are unable to face the risk of separation, and they therefore fight all their lives to keep from being dependent. They are those elusive persons who may even protect themselves by having many relationships, thus expressing a fundamental weakness: the impossibility of their living the relationship at a deep level with the accompanying necessity to fragment the experience in order to make it less painful. But this is the inevitable risk of existence: every relationship is born and is doomed to die.

At the moment of separation, the ego is not yet sufficiently strong and autonomous, exactly like the child who, though in the process of being separated from the mother, cannot survive without her care. The strengthening of the ego and the achievement of independence pass through another mythological and psychological stage, that of the hero's victorious struggle against the regressive forces of the unconscious, often represented by the image of the dragon. For it to be possible to undertake psychologically the adventure of the hero, whereby the ego is solidly structured through overcoming a series of difficult and perilous trials, detachment from the primary relation must take place without excessive perturbations that could lead to extreme reactions or to an actual foundering into the unconscious. The ego's weakness in this phase is spontaneously balanced by defensive attitudes, which operate in line with the successive development, but can also flow over into pathology if accentuated too much.

One of these mechanisms is the devaluation of emotions and feeling, which are the expression of that deep sphere linked to the unconscious, and as such dangerous for a consciousness that is not yet solidly established. Indeed, emotionality has a disintegrating power over consciousness, which is based instead on an objective view of things. For instance, if a child becomes aggressive and furious while listening to melting music, this behavior tesitifes to the immaturity of his ego, which feels threatened by anything that may arouse in him emotions he finds difficult to control. But if repression of the emotional sphere is too massive and persists as well into adult life, this signifies that the ego's development has not followed a normal course, and the apparent strength of the imperturbable and withdrawn person is only the mask for an intrinsic weakness that makes it impossible for him to let himself go in any kind of emotion or feeling.

The excessive accentuation of the ego, within certain limits, is normal and necessary at this stage, and is expressed in a narcissistic overevaluation of itself and the total negation of the unconscious. But it can be compensated by an opposite attitude, namely, as Neumann points out, "by a depressive self-destruction which, in the form of *Weltschmerz* [romantic discontent] and self-hatred, often culminates in suicide, all these being characteristic symptoms of puberty."[50] In other words, it is possible for the individual to perceive his own weakness too intensely and to feel himself overwhelmed by the world, to the point of actively seeking his own destruction in suicide.

Between these two extremes there exists an infinite range of gradations, marking in particular the psychology of adolescence.

The difficulties encountered in this phase justify its being compared to a psychotic condition: in the psychotic, as in the adolescent, a stable ego structure is completely lacking, something that makes psychological work with these patients extremely complex.

Let us now examine by what psychological and mythological stages the development of consciousness proceeds. We can say in general that the growth of the ego, after detachment from the original matrix, takes place through *incorporation* mechanisms, that is, apparently destructive acts that tend to fragment the still outside world in order gradually to assimilate and come to know it. This assimilation and knowledge are expressed, at this level, by an alimentary symbolism (to incorporate: to eat) not devoid of aggressive elements. This is understandable when we stop to think that our first relation with the outside world, and thus our first learning experience is the act of sucking and ingestion. Sometimes the sudden increase of hunger in a small child expresses symbolically the intensification of this incorporating activity, just as reading and avid studying do in a later phase. Expressions like "to devour books" preserve at the linguistic level this fundamental alimentary metaphor connected with knowledge.

Eating and biting are thus primary modalities of control and acquisition of whatever is extraneous to and different from ourselves, and we find them again in many aspects of our adult life — in the erotic sphere, for example, where it would be overly reductive to identify certain aggressive oral expressions like biting as simply a form of sadism. Indeed, it is possible that the biting exchanged by sexual partners in moments of greater abandon may even express an attempt to incorporate and know the other, and thus to overcome the fear of difference.

Extremely frustrated persons may develop a pathological voracity in a desperate attempt to dominate through food a world that in practice is being denied. This is the psychological dynamic that explains many cases of obesity.

This profound symbolic significance confers on the act of eating a ritual character, which even today continues to have great importance. The modern custom of fast food and eating on the run can be very harmful, not so much on the physiological plane as on the psychological one, since by reducing the meal to its literal and concrete purpose one completely loses the metaphorical meaning needed for the nourishment of the soul.

It is above all in this phase that the fundamental difference emerges in male and female experience, of which we have already spoken. After an initial period of total fusion and undifferentiation, the first appearance of consciousness and the ego involves, along with the separation of the parents and the emergence of the male-female polarity, a splitting of the psychic system into conscious and unconscious. In this phase, everything feminine and maternal is identified with the unconscious, while consciousness acquires a masculine character. Writes Neumann:

> The stage of separation of the World Parents which initiates the independence of the ego and consciousness by giving rise to the principle of opposites is therefore also the stage of increasing masculinity. Ego consciousness stands in manly opposition to the feminine unconscious.[51]

While the little boy perceives the ''masculinity'' of consciousness as something that belongs to him and with which it is easy to identify, the little girl, although she follows this same model in her development, feels as her own the ''femininity'' of the unconscious and finds it more difficult to identify totally with a masculine consciousness.

This can have very important psychological consequences. The radical differentiation that the man performs — and is helped to perform — between consciousness and the unconscious, and the total repression of the irrational sphere, have surely given rise to the highest cultural achievements. It is undeniable that science has a purely masculine connotation, but it is also undeniable that to this hubris of consciousness can be attributed the breakdowns that civilization itself has produced in the world and in man, uprooting him beyond measure from his natural instinctive base. Woman, on the other hand, who has preserved in the course of her personal and transpersonal history a greater permeability in relation to the influences of the unconscious, has a very deep perception of things, which is expressed in a modality quite alien to the male.

Thus, notwithstanding their capacity for objectification, and perhaps because of it, men have always demonstrated a certain immaturity in the sphere of human relations, a sphere that, beginning with the first phases of development of the masculine, is considered an unforgivable weakness and therefore devalued defensively along with everything that pertains to the unconscious and to the "feminine." Women have paid a concrete price for this psychological situation, and suffered an age-old oppression. The important thing, which is also the fundamental message of depth psychology, is to realize the necessity of bringing these two modalities of existence closer together, and not to set them against each other in a sterile dispute over which has the greater validity. Men and women have much to teach each other in order to try to achieve that state of psychological androgyny of which the Platonic myth speaks, where the capacity for relationship and the tendency to explore coexist in a creative dialectic within the individual.

Myths describing the earliest phases of existence, whether on the ontogenetic or phylogenetic plane, have a cosmic and impersonal character that makes it very difficult to translate them into the terms of an individual experience. This is understandable, in that they refer to a preconscious phase of humanity, in which the individual is still totally immersed in nature, and the ego in the unconscious. The great cosmogonies express by impersonal metaphors an experience that has never taken place, that is, an existential condition in which an ego capable of conscious perception is completely absent:

> The dawn state of the beginning projects itself mythologically in cosmic form, appearing as the beginning of the world, as the mythology of creation. Mythological accounts of the beginning must invariably begin with the outside world, for world and psyche are still one. There is as yet no reflecting, self-conscious ego that could refer anything to itself, that is, reflect.[52]

When, however, with the detachment from the uroboros and the separation of the parents, a first nucleus of the ego is affirmed and man begins to set himself up as an individual against internal and external transpersonal forces, the myth too takes on a personal form in which it becomes easiser to recognize our identity as human beings. The birth of ritual in this phase is the expression of man's first affirmation in the face of nature. In his rituals, writes Neumann, man "makes himself the responsible center of the cosmos; on him depends the rising of the sun, the fertility of crops, and all the doings of the gods."[53]

Here, with the differentiation from the original matrix, begins the *myth of the hero*, which describes in its various phases the long and difficult process of the ego's emancipation from the unconscious and represents the exemplary path that each individual must follow for the development of personality. In other words, the myth of the hero forms part of the individual development of each of us, and in the course of our existence it is always possible to discern its images. To know the meaning of the mythological elements that touch us most closely is extremely important if we are to understand certain personal experiences, whether real or imaginary, that have their roots in a deep psychic dimension, the one that guides our development in accordance with archetypal models common to all humanity.

"Unhappy is the land that needs a hero," sighs Brecht's Galileo,[54] but the desire for a life without heroism is a utopian and not a realistic wish. Clinical experience has constantly confirmed that the myth of the hero represents the fundamental structure of human life. Understanding this structure in childhood becomes therefore of prime importance. Dependence on the parents, particularly the mother in one's first years, develops, as we have already seen, a feeling of security toward life since its dangers are mediated and filtered. The child's condition does not allow it to face the world by itself, and so it must delegate this thankless task to others. While from the standpoint of biological survival this delegating is entirely functional, it becomes a little less so from the psychological standpoint since it delays for a long time one's understanding that external reality is absolutely indifferent to our fate, but is only what it is: something to be conquered as one conquers an object. This simple observation cannot be clear to the still small child who is living thanks to the protection of its family. It will become obvious only when one enters into adult life and understands to his or her sorrow that the world does not give itself spontaneously but must be taken.

To avoid misunderstanding, one should specify that the modalities of this conquest can only be strictly individual. Already in 1921 Jung, in calling the attention of scholars to two fundamental attitudes, extroversion and introversion, emphasized that one should not see in the extroverted modality the only possibility of rapport with the world. In other words, whether it takes place by an inner or an outer search, what matters is to reach a precise awareness of one's own objectives, and when this happens (and the sooner the better, for the psychic health of the individual) all the obstacles that we meet will be seen as structural components of the same searching process, and not as malevolence on the part of the world.

But what does clinical experience unfailingly teach us? We increasingly learn that neurotic suffering is linked to a disturbing vision in which the world appears as an indestructible and everlasting enemy. The dynamic dimension of the object, whether internal or external, is completely repressed and replaced by an ironclad rigidity. The hero of the myth is above all *action*, just as in Hegel's words, "the force of mind is only as great as its expression,"[55] and every successful analysis constellates in the patient the myth of the hero.

One of the characterisitcs of the mythical hero is his double lineage: alongside the real parents there is always a supernatural father or mother. The Christian religion offers a very clear example of this in the figure of Christ, the son of God. The heroes of Greek mythology are likewise always sons of some deity. These are the unconscious antecedents behind the common custom of appointing godparents.

How many times have we imagined or heard of children imagining that their actual parents were not their real ones?[56] It happens often enough and, according to Neumann, indicates the activation of the archetypal image of the hero's "dual nature." This is an image that has its deep roots in the prepatriarchal experience of birth, when there was as yet no knowledge of the causal link between sexual relations with a man and the procreation of a child. Thus "It is not the man who is father to the child: the miracle of procreation springs from God."[57] This type of experience was particularly accentuated with the birth of a male child, that is, in the face of "the miracle that a female is able to produce a male out of herself. This miracle was, as we know, originally ascribed by primitive woman to the *numinosum*, to the wind or the ancestral spirits."[58]

In successive modifications of the myth, accompanying the advent of patriarchy, other factors contribute to the experience of the hero's dual nature. In the first place, there is the collective itself, the social context of the individual that considers him a hero, a rebel or anyway "different," because he deviates from the norm. His thinking and behavior are different with respect to the community; and then there is also the individual himself who perceives his own outsider status in relation to others and their values. Here emerge both the requirement for and experience of a superpersonal father as opposed to the earthly one, who is in fact the bearer of those values the hero is destined to combat.

We have all experienced times in which we realize, often with fear or disappointment, that others no longer understand us. But this, far from being a negative fact, is a sign of our emancipation, of our psychological development. Indeed, if we were always to be understood, it would mean that we were speaking the language of others, a collective language. But if our attitude and ideas are original, we can no longer be understood since we are expressing something new. Hence a feeling of mutual estrangement, whereby our search for an individual path is considered at least as "strange."

In these moments of development, it is our family that represents the collective, the given reality opposed to the growth of the individual. Open as it may be to the emergence of the new, it is nevertheless inevitable that the older generation is oppressive in relation to the younger, since the former lacks the experiences that would allow it to see things in a new way. For this reason, the personal father often appears in the myth as an opposing figure alongside the divine father.

The hero's fate is thus one of isolation, which is perceived as something both good and bad.

> The necessary thing is after all but this: solitude, great inner solitude. Going-into-oneself and for hours meeting no one — this one must be able to attain. To be solitary, the way one was solitary as a child.[59]

This counsel by Rilke suggests a fundamental psychological problem — the transition from the collective dimension to the individual one. It is a transition which, as one might imagine, carries a very high price, since the achievement of individuality can only take place by such means as we find within ourselves. This moment may coincide with an intense ostracism on the part of others, to whom we become incomprehensible, but it is precisely this incomprehension that constitutes the suffering that inevitably accompanies our attempt to formulate what by definition is indescribable. As an analyst, I must be aware of the fact that I am leading the patient toward an irreversible solitude, since those who have tasted the fruit of the tree of good and evil generally do not turn back. But what a difference there is between an imposed solitude and a solitude born within the sphere of an inner search! The one is meaningless, the other has meaning and, though painful, sets before our eyes the path of hope and rebirth. "Each stands alone at the heart of the earth/pierced by a ray of sunlight/and suddenly it's evening."[60]

The ray of sunlight is undoubtedly the awareness that sets us apart from others, as well as the arrow that painfully wounds us. Indeed, every awareness is peculiarly personal. And in the encounter with the patient I must constantly compare his journey with my own, in order to keep the two paths from merging in some way. Mindful of this danger, I remember one of my own dreams: "On my dining-room table lie three objects, one of them insignificant. But an inner voice tells me that it is precisely to the least important things that one must pay attention."

We should be aware that it is not infrequent in the course of an analysis for the assimilation of unconscious contents to drive the patient toward a maniacal condition, or rather toward a psychic inflation. In Arion's case I was uncertain whether this would happen, and so the dream that came to mind can be interpreted as a modest warning. (Freud: "One must guard against accepting flattery at its face value.")[61] What is conspicuous sometimes conceals deception while, as Hexagram 57 in the *I Ching* says, there is "success in small matters."[62] In my sessions with Arion I was perfectly aware of my wish that he emerge from the condition of stasis in which he found himself and resume a creative existence, but precisely because of the presence of this wish I had to be extremely cautious in my reactions and interpretations. As Heraclitus says, "The waking have one common world, but the sleeping turn aside each into a world of his own."[63]

And it is this inner world, "of his own," that I must respect so as to avoid the risk of having the cure of the patient coincide with an acceptance of my psychological system. I think this problem has been expressed with great clarity by W. M. Kranefeldt, a pupil of Jung:

> The danger deriving from the fact that every theory in its application "has its obvious premise in practice" is clearly this: that the solutions sought for problems of practical psychotherapy shift imperceptibly to the side of the will, and therefore, psychologically, are resolved in the continued exercise of certain orientations, which on the basis of certain affirmations, i.e., of the special content of the theory, are brought to the soul from outside instead of emerging from within the soul.[64]

One has to understand the temptation that the analyst must resist: that of using, sometimes out of sheer laziness or unconsciousness, an example of interpretation by which to assert his will to power over the patient. The history of every man, and thus also of the patient sitting before me, is the history of his problems. If I want to understand him fully, I must show him and myself where his problem lies. And the problem is never banal, while the way in which it is hidden from consciousness often is. The effort to get along on one's own, leading a simple, dull existence and thinking only of oneself, may be merely the reflex of a soul tormented from within and hoping to find relief in external success.

The problem is precisely that inner torment, and the response to the patient's suffering can come only through a discourse consistent with his psychological complexity. The response must thus arise from his own soul.

4

Psychic Reality

It has already been stressed that the value of the myth lies in the fact that it offers us once again, beyond narrative differences due to environmental and cultural factors, a model in which it is possible to recognize our own psychological complexity. And it is precisely in our own experience that the myth constantly comes back to life and unveils its meaning. In the mythologies of all times and places, the hero is called upon to perform exploits according to a specific archetypal pattern, and we must always ask ourselves what, in our present reality, are the heroic tasks demanded by our particular psychological situation if we are to proceed along the path of development.

Jung frequently points out the dangers present in the collision with the unconscious and the difficulties of assimilating it. How does one bring about diffusion between consciousness and the unconscious?

> This opens up the whole problem of translation into contemporary language, and perhaps the creation of a new language altogether. Thus we come back to the question of *Weltanschauung* — a *Weltanschauung* that will help us to get into harmony with the historical man in us.[65]

What is the myth that the patient lives in his analytic adventure, and I along with him? When an analysis begins, the archetypal motif behind the myth of Oedipus, that is, of consciousness, is generally constellated; the same motif underlies the myth of Theseus, who penetrates the labyrinth. This means that anyone who undertakes an analysis, even or especially if he has been driven to his knees by suffering and necessity and is initially unaware of what awaits him, chooses the path of deep awareness, which in itself is already a heroic act in that it requires one to achieve a relative view of consciousness and of the rational attitude predominant in our historical period. A withdrawal of energy from the outside world is also necessary, and for this a certain price must always be paid.

What, we might ask at this point, is the heaviest burden on our shoulders in these moments? Though admittedly one cannot generalize it is possible to single out the most painful thorn as it shows up in human relations. When one sets out on the road to inner awareness, the attitudes of others, especially in their rational expression, become increasingly transparent. Never, however, is it possible to unmask the haughty self-assurance of those who conceal their inner insecurity behind a seemingly logical discourse. This can only lead to painful moments, for although to us the other's unconsciousness, immaturity or lack of an encompassing vision of the world may be clear, it is impossible to communicate such truths to the intractable rational mind. One would find oneself up against a stone wall or even a threat of ruthless violence. The arrogance of insecurity prefers destruction to the charity that lies at the base of consciousness, but *"Non intratur in veritatem nisi per charitatem"* (You do not reach truth except through charity).[66]

The basic point in the analytic itinerary is precisely the confrontation with the unconscious, i.e., with the world that eludes the possibility of a rational interpretation. This is a factor that already by itself is enough to arouse fear, but there is also another aspect, one that is usually not sufficiently stressed, and that is the real and deep confrontation with the world and with ourselves. Analysis, in fact, teaches us not to assign responsibility for our difficulties to the outside world, but to take them upon our own shoulders. In other worlds, analysis reveals the cracks in our existence, and throws doubt on everything we have laboriously constructed and on which we have based our identity. Normally we are the result of an external effort of education, and this gives us a certain appearance with which we identify. Our lives are virtually constructed by others and by the educational principles that we unconsciously make our own. One of the first important steps of analysis is precisely the demolition of this construction and the laying bare of our existence. It is a necessary passage toward psychological understanding in depth, which cannot be accomplished on the intellectual plane but only through a personal experience involving the emotional sphere. Here is how one of Arion's dreams expresses this:

> I am clinging to a rocky vertical wall, in whose recesses I find some eggs. So as not to fall, I take hold of two eggs to right and left. I would also like to climb down, but I don't have the courage. I then ask help from a couple of acquaintances, a man and a woman. I realize that there are other eggs, but on looking closely I discover that they are all open, empty and broken.

One hardly needs to be a psychologist to understand a dream of this kind. To find oneself on a rocky cliff clearly indicates that one is in trouble, and the pair of acquaintances suggests once again the parents, to whom one turns for help in moments of danger. Then the dreamer sees broken, empty eggs: what ought to contain life in reality contains nothing. Perilous situations had also appeared previously, but now for the first time the patient dreams of finding himself with nothingness in his hands and he is forced to face up to his own failure. There is no need for communication of a verbal and logical kind to make him understand the dream message, since at the emotional level the metaphor is completely transparent.

Faced with such a tragic image, one might be excused for wondering whether Arion will ever succeed in making progress, and particularly in not breaking down. It is in moments like these that counter-transference factors—that is, the analyst's emotional response to the patient's vital problem, which inevitably constellates in the analyst as well the same problematic knots—assume a particular importance. For the patient to be able to face his own inner void, it is necessary for the analyst to be able to grasp deeply both the patient's message and its relevance for himself on the psychological plane. During that session, while I was in a state of "fluctuating attention,"[67] a dream came back to me, one I had had at the age of five and which I had spoken of in my own analysis:

> I was in Rome, in the EUR district, and as I was walking the ground under my feet turned into quicksand, and I fell into it. I told myself that I must get out of it as quickly as possible and woke up in a state of anxiety.

My analyst asked me what I associated with the EUR district, and I answered that it had been built by Mussolini, that is to say by a person representing power and arrogance. He then asked me how I stood in relation to power, for the dream clearly had to do with my psychological situation when I was a child, that is, with problems of inferiority that had driven me to seek a compensation in power. But such a life style continually threatens to engulf one in quicksand; it is a superstructure created to save oneself, but in reality it destroys the individual. Thus, in the presence of a patient who speaks to me of his failure by means of a dream, my inner resonance evokes a problem of power. Arion's dream arouses in me this echo, so I can also suppose that power enters into his problem, the problem of a successful man who feels himself to be a failure. It may be that only a need for power has driven him to do certain things, with the result that his accomplishments do not correspond to his individual essence. Hence the gap between what he seems to be and what he actually is.

The patient perceives empathically my participation in the discovery of failure when faced with the image of the empty eggshells, and feels that I may be able to help him because I myself succeeded in extricating myself from that quicksand. This means that the real therapeutic means is not technical, but is based on the capacity to create a psychological field in which two individuals truly face each other, albeit at different levels of awareness and communication, in order to face the patient's deep wounds together.

The validity of the interpretation in terms of power is confirmed by a later dream, which echoes the difficulties of the previous one, but presents them in a very different context. This indicates that mutual activation sets in motion psychological mechanisms that work to repair the situation in which we find ourselves and of which the dream offers an incredibly precise snapshot. But a snapshot portrays a particular moment and not a fixed and unchanging situation. What is important is to grasp together with the patient not so much the block or the difficulties, but rather the transformations, slight as they may be, that indicate an ongoing process.

In the new dream Arion finds himself in a car with a friend:

> The friend asks me to make a detour, which I would prefer not to do. But I agree, and at dusk we reach a town. There is a twisting road that leads down into the valley and then up again on the other side. In the town there are many little intersecting streets, as well as some difficult thoroughfares, and I suffer from dizziness. A space that looks wide enough to pass through becomes narrower as we approach. We do not know whether to keep going or to turn back. Suddenly I wake up.

The structure of the little town, with all those intersecting streets, calls to mind the archetypal image of the labyrinth, which fundamentally expresses the path of life. Indeed, our existence, if it is to proceed individually and responsibly, cannot be linear as is commonly believed: a life lived in an authentically human way requires continual choices among various directions and different possibilities. This naturally includes the risk of detours and mistakes, not to mention losing one's way, but the acceptance of this risk is the necessary condition for the search for an individual path. Many myths speak of the labyrinth, but the most famous is surely the Cretan one, where Theseus with the help of Ariadne kills the Minotaur, the maternal monster that the hero must destroy if he is not instead to be destroyed by it.

In short, the labyrinth represents a crucial moment. As Colli remarks:

> The geometric form of the Labyrinth, with its unfathomable complexity, invented through a bizarre and perverse game of the intellect, alludes to the ruin, to the mortal peril that lies in wait for man when he dares to confront the animal-god.[68]

We should be very clear about the "mortal peril" of analysis. The crux of the matter lies hidden in the fact that in the first phases of the treatment all our psychological defenses are, so to speak, dismantled. To give an example, they are equivalent to the body's immune defenses against disease. When we experience a loss of defenses, we have no reference points and we are *truly* lost inside our labyrinth of drives. At this point the labyrinth itself becomes a constant problem that man puts to himself. No longer the security of the unconscious, but the fragility and uncertainty of consciousness. This is why at these moments it is so difficult to live; this is why one is at the mercy of the aggressiveness of others, who mistake for hesitation what is merely critical reflection. These are delicate situations that Arion must now face, also because his suffering is echoed by the unassuaged memory of the same difficulty that I had to go through when, my own soul wounded, I sought the light of consciousness not by attacking the world but by tormenting myself. This condition is familiar in analysis, and justifies James Hillman's assertion that "the so-called counter-transference is actually prior to transference."[69]

Precisely because the analyst's attitude, apart from anything in the individual patient, is already working to activate a search for consciousness, Hillman calls this situation "the engendering of soul through love."[70]

To state that the countertransference is the basis of the analytic relationship, and that in reality it represents the alpha and omega of the process, means to have actually understood what analysis is all about. Against this thesis, those who *play* the analyst instead of *being* analysts hurl themselves in vain. Those who play the analyst, indeed, have not the slightest perception of the importance of their involvement, and they continually and in a mistaken fashion nail the patient to his past. The countertransference truly "acquires its truest dimension only through comparison with the inner entreaties issuing from the analytic situation."[71]

This therefore is why the analytic experience with a patient constantly re-evokes in me the path I have traveled from childhood to the present. But it is just this familiar path that puts me in the condition of the castaway who turns to gaze on dangerous water, in order to release the sense of fullness and vital impact for one who comes to me for help.

But let us return to Arion's dream. With respect to the preceding one, it expresses a qualitative leap of great importance: in the first there are fear, blockage, broken eggs; in the second the dreamer finds himself in a dynamic situation, one of movement. Danger, however, is still present: Theseus, too, found himself in danger, but succeeded in killing the Minotaur and emerging from the labyrinth, *with the help of a woman*.

In the structure of myths there is always a feminine element that furnishes decisive help for the completion of the task. As we know, Ariadne was later betrayed and abandoned by Theseus (the still fickle and restless male), but the archetypal model always shows that the female furnishes the thread of existence and gives it meaning. I must therefore ask myself where Arion's feminine element is, and what are his relations with it and with women in general.

Here opens a painful chapter in this man's life. I am usually reluctant to speak of the concrete aspects of personal life, because these are not the cause of one's troubles. They do, however, help us to understand, since they are in any case the mirror of an inner situation. James Hillman, in a private communication, once pointed out to me that "all marriages are a mistake," and by putting this sentence between quotation marks, invited me to grasp its symbolic meaning. It is very hard for two spouses to show a parallel psychological development, particularly because of the different stimulations that society itself offers men and women. Sooner or later they always end by being strangers, since each has followed his or her own path. Social pressure, and above all the presence of children, ensure that two people will go on living together even when they have nothing more to say to each other. This is understandable on the sociological plane, but absurd and inadmissible on the psychological one.

Arion had married a woman who in effect acted as his mother. There was no passion in him; the maternal female image does not arouse him and offers only security and protection. Choosing a partner of this kind, whether on the part of the man or the woman, means choosing death, since security is only an appearance that conceals psychic death, which contaminates every aspect of our existence. It is not possible to be alive on the plane of intelligence and dead on that of feeling, for emotion and intellect are closely linked. The condition of psychic death makes our thought sterile, crystallizing it in stereo-typed patterns, even when it seems to be adapting itself to external reality.

The patient is thus a person who, having had certain experiences at the personal level, takes upon himself again, in marriage, a false rela-tionship in which there is nothing to be expressed. The female part-ner becomes a "mother" to him and takes on herself all the aspects of this problem.

We do not know if and when "Ariadne" will appear in his life, but we do know that in fairytales the good fairy or helpful animal turns up when the hero performs an act of courage. It is an illusion to think that help is necessary before we can make a move: generally the op-posite is true, and the assisting forces intervene at the moment when we face up to the dangers. Thus, in our lives, an act of courage can be the premise for the meeting with a new person.

At the end of the session we parted with no certainty, but with the hope that sooner or later Ariadne would appear. Since the myth cor-responds to the mysteries of life, we must understand what the help of a maiden or nymph, a princess or goddess, means on the psycho-logical plane.

According to analytical psychology, the appearance of Ariadne, the outer woman who lends help to the hero, expresses the possibility of a collaborative relationship between the masculine ego and the inner feminine image, which Jung calls the anima. The act of courage, by which the hero penetrates the labyrinth and confronts the Minotaur, transforms the conscious attitude, and this transformation is connected with the encounter with the inner feminine element, that is, with a dimension other than the usual one of consciousness and the ego.

We might now ask ourselves whether in order to reach this inner dimension it is necessary or indispensable to have a concrete relation-ship with a person in the real world. On the theoretical plane, we should have to answer no, in that it would seem possible to know one's own inner dimension at a purely symbolic, endopsychic level. In practice, however, it is invariably the real experience of the femi-nine (or of the masculine, in the case of a woman) that constellates our inner reality and allows us to perceive it.

Roughly speaking, we can say that the appearance in the myth of a female partner for the hero represents, on the phylogenetic plane, the birth of the man as an individual, that is, the passage from the matriarchal phase to the patriarchal one, in which the female is no longer the *impersonal* matrix of life and death, but a *personal* element with which the more mature ego can enter into rapport through the concrete and personal relation with a woman. On the individual psychological plane — as we see, for example, in analysis — this female figure represents instead the rapport with the inner reality of the anima, which has only a projective link with persons in real life.

We have thus entered the phase of development in which the hero, having divided the uroboric situation into father and mother, consciousness and the unconscious, must at a certain point confront the split that he himself has caused. In fairytales, the hero typically wins the princess or treasure through a combat, which signifies that interiority is the prize for those who succeed in accomplishing the heroic feat. As Lévi-Strauss also shows,[72] the recurrent model is that the princess is given as a bride to the winner of a tourney or test of astuteness. But whatever may be the deed to be accomplished, the hero always puts his own life in jeopardy: the alternative to winning the princess is thus psychic death.

What does all this mean psychologically? It means that in our psychological development, in order to be able to seize and reintegrate that aspect that we have neglected because of a one-sided upbringing of the man-man and woman-woman type, whereby men repress the feminine element and women the masculine, a combat is necessary, a heroic exploit. But against what or whom must we fight?

In the course of growing older, we all pass from a situation of complete adherence to our parents to gradually but inexorably taking a stand against them. It is also possible to see how looking at one's parents with suspicion coincides with the projection of one's own psychic dimension onto the face of a woman or man. The discovery of love and one's first erotic experiences have an immediate connection with this questioning of the parents, for it is often at these very moments that one begins to lie, and lying is already a form of struggle.

In all mythologies, the hero's combat displays two different but equally important aspects, which we can sum up under the headings "killing of the mother" and "killing of the father." On the plane of our personal experience, this double killing is equivalent to weakening the parental figures until we arrive at a situation in which their words leave us totally indifferent. This is the great discovery that each of us makes when he or she is truly grown up in relation to the parents. If in our adult lives a word from the father or mother still hurts us — or even makes us feel good — this means that we are not sufficiently detached from the childhood dimension of dependence.

Parents represent protection by those who nourish us and hold a lantern that lights our path, since they themselves have already traveled it. It thus takes great courage to say no to these persons.

In practice, everyone in analysis finds himself facing this separation. Indeed, his psychic discomfort derives from a profound contradiction: that of stretching forward while having on his shoulders the enormous weight of values that have had their consistency and validity, but now are obsolete. The persistence of these values and the power of those who offer them to us are proportionate to our inability to see ahead. In other words, it is as though they were trying to sell us an old model of a car, one already tested but by now inadequate for our needs, and we should have to struggle to buy a new model suitable to ourselves — a situation in fact frequently depicted in dreams.

The analyst, however, is always aware that deeper attitudes, anchored in one's earliest experiences, cannot be so easily transformed, unlike, for instance, the mental acquisition of technical information, which can always supplant previous knowledge. Emotion has very deep roots and only other emotions can be juxtaposed to it. To a man who loves, you cannot speak with reason, but only with love. As I have already said, dreams are generally the chief instrument within the analytic discourse, since they have the aroma of an "irrational truth" that agitates us to our roots and "tells" us different things. Note also that it is the analytic situation itself that in many cases facilitates the memory of dreams, and even provokes them, just as incubation at Epidaurus activated healing dreams.[73]

The interpretation of dreams during analysis does not involve merely a rational communication of psychological meanings, but also an emotional expectation of the responses that the patient's unconscious itself will give to our words and hypotheses. This attitude on the part of the analyst functions as a stimulus; it is as though we were to put viruses into the other that then do their work. If the patient and I are compatible, there is the possibility of growth; otherwise there will be a rejection. Just as the transplanting of physical organs presupposes an identity of structure, so it is in analysis. If the analyst and the patient have things to say to each other, the virus catches on and dreams and drawings will show this; that is, the unconscious will indicate the journey we are undertaking together. If instead there is no communication at the deeper levels of our psyches, there is rejection; the patient will continue to be sick or will make no progress. Let us see how Arion's unconscious expresses itself at this point in the analysis:

> I dream that my navel itches; I look at it, see that it is dirty, and try to clean it with a matchstick. To facilitate the operation, I smooth the skin around the navel with my left hand, but I make a mistake and see the navel emerge as though it were detaching itself. I am worried and also realize that it looks like a cooked fava bean. Then I wake up.

This is a complex dream since it can be seen on at least two different levels, and the therapist must have sufficient sensitivity to grasp the element that will make it possible to go ahead. The patient, then, detaches his own navel, but in the dream he also thinks of a fava bean, and this by association has another significance, since in Italian *fava* is a vulgar word for the penis. I thus have two clear references: the cutting of the umbilical cord and castration. These two aspects are both present in the psychic situation described in the dream and perfectly express the ambivalence typical of every phase of psychological development.

As I have already said, every forward impulse is accompanied by the echo of an attachment to the past, and this is what makes us experience each of our acts of liberation as dangerous. But if in a situation like this I were to stress the reductive aspect, attachment to the past, I would only be reinforcing the patient's conscious attitude, his feelings of impotence and failure. My choice instead of the relatively more optimistic or purposive interpretation is not a deception, but a way of joining with the possibility of development offered by the dream itself. An absolutely impeccable interpretation on the theoretical plane — assuming such exists — might not be at all productive on the psychological plane. Had I not received and retransmitted the message of the dream in terms of its potential, had I dwelt instead on castration and fear, I would have been playing into the hands of the regressive forces in the unconscious.

Keeping in mind the struggle that Arion is engaged in to free his own individuality from the suffocating grasp of the parents, I can allow him to understand the myth that is being re-enacted in his psychological process and to realize as well that what he sees as "dirty" is precisely his struggle against the mother. There is a "divine" commandment to honor one's father and mother. But laws serve rather as a bulwark against forbidden impulses. Freud correctly observes that without laws all our lust and violence would be released. The prohibition thus makes it possible to shift our impulses onto a symbolic plane and to experience endopsychically, for example, the killing of the mother. Among other things, we see that in the dream he touches himself with his *left* hand, and the left is always linked to a dimension different from that of consciousness, which is oriented toward "objective" reality. It is therefore on a purely psychological plane that Arion is carrying out this metamorphosis and reliving the separation from the mother, despite the fact that he is no longer young.

But at the moment when the "killing of the mother" takes place, there is an immediate reaction by the "parents" against the son. This occurrence, which comes up again in every individual existence, is in reality transpersonal and belongs to man's phylogenetic development. Arion's next dream splendidly depicts the situation:

> I come upon two dogs, a male and a female, belonging to a friend of mine, and which usually greet me by wagging their tails. This time they growl at me, and I stop their growling by throwing into their jaws a wooden disk left over from the wood cut for the fireplace.

The wooden disk may remind us of a coin, in turn suggesting the image of Cerberus, the vicious hound of Hades who was pacified with a coin. But the most interesting thing about the dream is the dreamer's capacity to keep the dogs at bay. Indeed, he neither shows fear nor runs away, probably because the previous dream and the way we interpreted it together have allowed him to distance himself from what he obscurely feared. In reality fearful things do not exist, but only our fear, which is the manifestation of a particular attitude and a particular way of looking.

We are generally raised, often in subtle ways, to consider certain things objectively difficult and dangerous, and so we might say that analysis is a situation of re-education in which the individual takes advantage of his own strength and learns to see things with different eyes.

Here the process of struggle begins. In the myth, the hero must destroy the "father" and "mother," both often represented by the dragon. In Freud's reductive and causal conception, the struggle with the dragon is seen in purely personalistic terms, and thus related exclusively to a stage of childhood and to the concrete relationship with the parents. But the structure of the myth of the hero is always present in the course of our existence, with its three fundamental points: the *hero*, the evolving ego; the *dragon* to be fought, namely everything that stands opposed to individual growth; and the *treasure*, difficult to reach and appearing in the myth in various guises — the captive woman, the pearl, the water of life, the herb of immortality, etc. — which is always related to the birth of the new. Thus the hero's fight with the dragon is not simply performed once and for all at a particular moment in our development. As Neumann writes:

> The dragon fight is correlated psychologically with different phases in the ontogenetic development of consciousness. The conditions of the fight, its aim and also the period in which it takes place, vary. It occurs during the childhood phase, during puberty, and at the change of consciousness in the second half of life, wherever in fact a rebirth or a reorientation of consciousness is indicated. For the captive is the "new" element whose liberation makes further development possible.[74]

Every time life itself imposes on us a change in our mode of being, we find ourselves face to face with a "dragon" that guards our treasure and must be fought. In general, a person going into analysis seems to want to recover from life — that is, he wants neither the dragon nor the treasure. But the analyst knows that the true request involves life, because it is by gaining awareness that one attains a level of existence at which it is impossible to avoid struggle, and thus from passivity one passes to activity. Dragon and treasure then become the activating elements of consciousness. For example, peoples who conquer new lands are very different from those who live on mountaintops and devote themselves to raising sheep. Frontier people, in fact, always put their own lives in jeopardy; they are always face to face with their natural enemies and this impels them to make constant changes.

The struggle with the dragon is thus the central image of our rebirth, but it should not be understood, as in Freudian psychoanalysis, in merely personalistic and reductive terms, as the elimination of something real. In the archetypal view of Jungian psychology, the fight with the dragon, in its twofold aspect of "killing the mother" and "killing the father," represents the struggle against our unconscious being. To the sphere of the "mother" belongs, in Neumann's words, "any content that functions through its emotional dynamisms, such as the paralyzing grip of inertia or an invasion by instinct."[75] The world of the "father," on the other hand, is that of collective values:

a spiritual system which . . . captures and destroys the son's consciousness. This spiritual system appears as the binding force of the old law, the old religion, the old morality, the old order; as conscience, convention, tradition, or any other spiritual phenomenon that seizes hold of the son and obstructs his progress into the future.[76]

In the development of consciousness, it is the maternal dragon that must first be slain, through the active "incest" of the hero, who consciously penetrates the instinctual matrix and in this way acquires dominion over it. The symbolism of incest at this level thus takes on a progressive meaning, clearly differentiating itself by its active nature from the kind that appears in the uroboric and matriarchal phases. Uroboric incest, in fact, is the dissolution in the unconscious of a not yet differentiated ego, which lets itself be passively enveloped by the feminine element. In the matriarchal phase, the masculine ego begins to have a distinct existence of its own and to set itself against the maternal, but because of its own weakness in the face of a transpersonal and omnipotent feminine element, it is in constant danger of succumbing.

A characteristic symptom of this psychological condition is the fear of women, which may express itself in actual impotence. Every time we are consulted by a young man who suffers from this disturbance, we can observe that his greatest hope is that it is the result of physical causes. But in my experience physical impotence exists only in very rare cases; it has instead a particularly psychological basis. Impotence is the way in which the still immature male reacts to the fear he experiences in a feminine presence with which he is unable to come to terms. And it is thus a radical way of refusing a relationship in which the male feels overwhelmed. And so it does no good to go from one girl to another, since it is not the concrete woman who makes the male impotent, but the projection onto her of an originally unconscious dimension, which is feared as much as it may be desired.

An essential step for the stabilization of the masculine ego and consciousness is therefore that of the hero who confronts the power of the female (and of the unconscious), uniting with it in a generative incest that liberates the "fruitful and bountiful aspect"[77] from the maternal dragon.

5

The Destiny of Great Souls

In the last dream we saw how Arion was able to hold at bay two dogs, a male and a female, in which we recognized the paternal and maternal aspects of the unconscious, which he must confront if he is to make headway in his psychological development. We also proposed to interpret the dream image in mythical terms, as the beginning of the hero's journey toward the conquest of a treasure: a fantastic and symbolic journey that analytical psychology calls the process of individuation, leading to the discovery of one's own deeper values.

At this point one ought to stress the fact that when this confrontation begins it is almost inevitable that moments of depression will occur, which may be expressed in a wish to give up. Fairytales and myths often contain situations that the hero does not succeed in overcoming, but this experience, which might be seen as a structural reality of man, is particularly obvious in the analytical process, which is strewn with seemingly insurmountable obstacles. What can be done in such situations?

To answer this question, we might turn to a modern thinker, Antonio Gramsci, who has left us some highly illuminating thoughts on a fundamental polarity of existence, optimism and pessimism, that psychologically would seem to divide people into two opposite categories: those who pay no attention to obstacles and go forward in an a-critical and all-powerful way, and those who instead let themselves be stymied by the slightest difficulty.

Antonio Gramsci traveled a very painful road in fascist prisons, where his only relationship was with himself. His notebooks and letters, written in prison and published posthumously, are a profound testimony to it.[78] The letters in particular, being more intimate, are also much more revealing of his psychological attitude. In one of them, written in December 1929 to his brother Carlo, he declares that those "trite and vulgar states of mind known as pessimism and optimism" can arrive at a creative synthesis only if man achieves "the profound conviction that . . . he has within himself the source of his own moral strengths, and that everything depends on him, on

58

his energy, on his will.'' And he sums up his thought with a sentence from the French writer Romain Rolland: ''I am a pessimist with my intelligence, but an optimist by my will.''[79]

The pessimism of the intelligence is the fruit of a view of reality devoid of illusions; it is the ruthless awareness of obstacles that truly exist. The optimism of the will is specifically faith in the human possibility of facing obstacles while consciously running the risk of defeat. The hero is therefore someone who sees how things really are, but does not allow himself to be checked by them. This is basically the direction of analysis: it does not create illusions, but rather activates intrinsic pessimism in the understanding of life, while simultaneously nourishing and providing support and foundation for the optimism of the will.

In the analytic situation, when a moment of depression arrives and the patient is ready to give up the struggle, he or she is experiencing only one of these two poles. It is then up to the analyst to bring to the fore his faith that events in any case always depend on ourselves. It is like offering an elixir that makes it possible to go forward in spite of the difficulties. And in this way one comes to understand that nothing is beyond man and that obstacles basically cause us to become stronger. The analyst, by his silence and understanding, helps the suffering person to detach himself from a dimension of non-life, which is actually his own suffering: pessimism, the death of the will. Genuinely optimistic persons are by no means superficial, for they are precisely the ones who have understood the reality of things. Gramsci states that because he had never had any illusions, he was never disillusioned; this is the pessimism of the intelligence, which grants us the power to take on the world, something impossible for those who instead delude themselves and by mechanisms of negation refuse to see reality. Such individuals will be prey to disappointment and above all to a paralyzing pessimism.

At these moments, dreams take on great importance in the course of the analysis, since they reveal to us exactly how the patient is reacting at a deep level, whether there are dangers, and whether the analyst's contribution is a valid one. Let us therefore take a look at Arion's next dream:

> I steal a bus parked in front of my parents' house. After driving around for a while, I return to my point of departure. I then realize that those places where I spent my childhood have completely changed: instead

of poverty and squalor there are now fine buildings and clean streets — almost an air of luxury.

In order to throw light on certain aspects of the dream, it is necessary to keep in mind a few details concerning the dreamer's life. We already know that he is a man of culture and that he has achieved a certain external success, but he still carries within him the memory of his modest origins, the "poverty and squalor" to which the dream alludes. And here a large problem arises, one that we must often call attention to in analysis. It is the fact that we are much more conditioned by our early environment than we generally care to admit.

This does not mean that it is impossible to rise to higher levels, but simply that we always carry within us our basic condition, no matter what goal we may succeed in reaching. Social deliverance in the modern world generally occurs through study, but those who come from the socio-economic lower classes must make an enormous effort to bridge the gap and actually travel much farther than those who had been close to the goal since birth. Those who are born where no paths have been laid out go to immense difficulties to find their own. Unimaginable tears are shed in the course of their psychological journey by those who, lacking any support, have to create everything for themselves. It is like having to force one's way through a forest with one's bare hands.

Arion had personally experienced this very breach between social success and an inner despair that undermined any feeling of security about what he had achieved. Unless one has a solid social and cultural background, one always feels in danger and even in debt in the presence of life: it is as though everything we have, despite the efforts it has cost us, had been in some way given to us and could therefore be taken away at a moment's notice. One is then obliged to thank the good Lord daily for the very fact of survival, and if we also have success, there is an extremely acute feeling of not deserving it. This attitude of renunciation is imparted to us almost with our mother's milk, and remains within us like a negative imprinting that keeps us from enjoying our achievements.

But the patient's dream offers a new perspective. We see him committing a theft, which in mythology is always an act of courage, and this very act allows him to go back and extend his vision. Now he is able to realize that his poverty is over. Psychologically this means that his attitude has changed, and that the eyes with which he sees have been transformed. It is not an outer change that has taken place, but a structural transformation within himself. This is confirmed in the next dream:

> I realize that I have a very large penis, even though I do not have an erection. I am even unable at first to get it into my trousers; then with a little effort I manage to do so. A girl is watching with obvious pleasure, but this does not surprise me. What draws my attention instead is that my penis looks like a large pod slowly opening in the sun.

Leaving aside a literal interpretation, we can see the penis as a symbol of strength and fertility, as attested by ancient cults all over the world — in India, for example, or in ancient Rome, not to mention the Egyptian myth of Osiris, in which the god's phallus plays a central role. Even today this symbol shows its effectiveness by the naive attribution to the size of the penis of one's own sense of identity and virility. But if we avoid the banality of a literal connotation, we can give to the phallus a clear meaning of magnitude, strength and power; this is what Arion feels he has acquired, along with the possibility of not being ashamed of it.

The discovery and acceptance of his own creative power, which can be displayed and admired without fear, represent a crucial moment in our hero's psychological vicissitudes. As we have already seen, this man's difficulty lies in a lack of correspondence between his inner and outer states, in his being split in two, which makes his artistic production less rich than it might be and gives him a deep sense of failure. A possible explanation of the inability to demonstrate one's own values and richness, whereby even valuable persons fail to give concrete form to their creativity, lies, in my opinion, in a fundamental and structural fear of other people's envy. Aeschylus, in the *Agamemnon*, has Clytemnestra say that those who fear envy are in reality afraid to be great.[80]

To be creative, to carry the world forward by one's thought or by one's works, means to risk drawing down hatred on oneself, and only someone who is capable of withstanding it is able to say the right words. What prevents us from discovering ourselves, and from expressing our truth, is always the fear of losing other people's love. But if the purpose of life becomes that of gaining the love of others rather than seeking truth, our existence is reduced to a psychological conformism that does not allow us to express anything new.

Any man who thinks for himself and travels unbeaten paths provokes consternation and aggression, and becomes the target of abuse. In others he evokes desperate ghosts of ruin and transgression. In other words, his example bears witness to and inevitably signals the lack of soul in others. If it is true that "no one becomes a great man unless he has the courage to ignore a countless number of useless things,"[81] it is also true that self-realization, at whatever level it may occur, must be combined with a psychic power that very few people possess. How many intelligent minds and fantastic potentialities have I encountered in the course of my analytic practice, and how many times fear of the envy of others and the childish wish to preserve some impossible love lay at the origin of an unhappy psychic paralysis! As Dostoyevsky says:

> Everything is in man's hands and he lets everything pass in front of his nose and simply because of his cowardice. . . . It's strange, but what do men fear most of all? A new step, a new word of their own— that's what they mostly fear.[82]

Love of truth makes us state that the world is round or that a great many worlds exist. What is the price paid for making these statements? Columbus was put in chains, and Giordano Bruno paid for his intuition by being burned at the stake. These men and all those who pursue truth do not hide themselves, on the contrary they come into the light.[83] They are propelling mechanisms and dig paths for others, since actually, as Goethe points out:

> Truth always acts in a fruitful way and encourages those who possess and nourish it; error, on the other hand, remains lifeless and sterile, and indeed it may be thought of as a necrosis in which the part that perishes prevents the living part from healing.[84]

When we reflect on our experience, we realize that our tongues are often silent because to speak would mean to alienate other people's love and to draw down derision and hatred on ourselves. We can hypothesize that this inability to place oneself in conflict with others goes back to the early phases of development, when the need for love and protection is absolute and total. We have already said that to mature psychologically means to come to accept the negative, both outside and inside oneself, and this means to accept the aggressiveness of an other or indeed even his or her absence. When this does not happen, the typically childish fear of being abandoned remains in one's adult existence. We see it in persons who have an extreme need to be always surrounded by friends, obliging persons willing and able to do their utmost to keep the parental ties alive, precisely because they have been unable to accept the absence or aggressiveness of the mother. Such persons risk not being able to speak; they become in some way banal, because, in order to be able to say anything new, one must know how to undergo conflicts.

Aeschylus also says that few men are capable of loving, without envying, a friend whose destiny has been fortunate. The envious individual sees in the happiness of others a continuous curse on himself, and accordingly becomes imbued with poison: successful people are pursued by envy and this is something difficult to bear. Pasteur, for example, was hampered by the envy of doctors and had to give up his experiments for a certain length of time.[85]

All those who have something new to say pay the price of hatred and are subject to the law whereby no one is a prophet in his own country. Thus the fear of being creative has a structural foundation in the fear of envy. It is natural and correct to think of external envy, since envious persons really do exist and the persecution that they are able to inflict on us is real. But we should also realize that what actually paralyzes us is our own fear. Man's greatness thus passes through a confrontation with whatever opposes our creativity *from within*. The struggle conducted to assert and express oneself is never primarily external; what is essential instead is the resolution of inner conflicts, which are those that give others the possibility of injuring us, and above all take away our ability to express our true individuality. There are persons who become blocked even when they have to write a friendly letter; this happens because basically they are afraid of exposing themselves, at any level whatsoever. But as Nietzsche says: "*What does your conscience say?* — 'You shall become the person you are.' "[86]

These simple words bring forth the memories of an ancient wisdom that has always accompanied humanity at those moments when the question is raised about its meaning. But simple as they are, these words place every person in a serious and decisive situation of conflict. To become what we are means to have a creative and dynamic relationship with reality; it means above all to become different and capable of grasping certain flashes of truth. But why is all this difficult? Is it because for thousands of years the knowledge of self has been shot through with fear and trembling, while collectivization rises as sovereign with overwhelming force? It is necessary to understand how everyone who sets out on the road of his own destiny must reckon with the envy of others, a wholly special envy that Melanie Klein has masterfully described by tracing it back to its psychodynamic origins.[87]

Man's strength lies securely in the vigor of his ideas and these thoughts have the power to transform him completely. In the case of one whose existence has been silent for years, sudden inspiration is equivalent to having tapped a spring of cool fresh water that gushes violently from the rock. The sweetness of this water is so alluring that now it is necessary to make it gush forth continually. And even though slander is heavy to bear, and the poison that contaminates the discovery bitter, the strength of one's own soul can succeed in overcoming fear. Great souls suffer only when their greatness is derided.

Now I must release the patient from himself, from his fear. We have seen how Arion exposed himself in the last dream: his creative potential is now free of fear. At this moment I feel more certain, because the dream informs me that we are moving ahead and that I can now "push" if necessary. This means baring more and more the shadow aspects of his personality, knowing that now he can accept them, since he has a "penis" that no one will take away from him, which is to say he is ready to experience his own creativity without fearing the hatred of others.

Of course, I will still have to pay close attention to his reactions and weigh my interpretative attitude against his actual capacity for integration. And dreams, which carry the other's emotional response, are the essential instruments for this verification. Let us look at the dream that came next:

> I am on a mountain where there are construction sites and excavations. It is time to go down and return to the city. I realize, however, that the road is in poor shape, even though it can be traveled. I am all confused, and the road winds between precipices to left and right. But despite it all I am able to proceed, and at the moment I start off I see that there is a reassuring parapet all along the descending road. In this way I reach the city.

In the metaphor of the dream we can see with fair certainty the analytic process we are going through, and the readiness, as well as the necessity, to deepen it further. In a previous dream, Arion had been blocked with a car in a small town. There too there had been precipices over which he could have fallen, and I had associated this situation with the image of Theseus entering the labyrinth. In this case, although the danger is similar, the dreamer does not stop but continues to descend despite his fear. Through the analytic relationship, through the support and encouragement furnished by the analyst, a profound need to come to terms with himself is set in motion in the patient: he *must* go ahead, and at that moment he also realizes that he *can*. Indeed, there is a "reassuring parapet" that allows him to descend.

This dream assures me that a psychological structure, activated by our relationship, has been established in him, making him capable of carrying the process forward, facing its dangers and finding himself. In other words, the analyst offers the individual the opportunity to build self-immunizing and self-repairing structures within himself. This is the essential function of the dream. Suggestions and advice from the outside are actually of no use, since the only valid response is the one that stems from our personal psychological complexity.

The image of a solar phallus, along with a woman who looks at it with admiration and without any feeling of fear, expresses the overcoming of the Terrible Great Mother, which is to say the state of profound unawareness on which our consciousness stands rooted and into which it can fall at any moment. At this point new opportunities arise for exploration and relationship, both external and internal—in other words, one is ready for the exploits that at the mythological level are the equivalent of the "killing of the father."

At the beginning of the analytic relationship, the patient is an unconscious person, unaware of his inner conflict; all he sees is an obstacle or an *external* enemy. The function of the analysis lies precisely in destroying this paranoiac attitude, and letting the patient see that the outer world structures itself in terms of his inner dimension. If a change takes place within the personality, external facts lose their power to do harm, since this depends simply on the presence of weak points in ourselves. A classic example would be those persons who are said to be "unlucky in love": it is generally not a question of bad luck at all, but of a psychological problem involving the emotional sphere and which, so long as it remains unconscious, operates as an actual conditioning that drives these individuals always to choose the wrong partners.

One must nevertheless keep in mind that in the early stages of the analytic process, even if the person *wants* to gain awareness of these things, it is not easy to communicate them to him, nor would it be psychologically desirable. Indeed, any knowledge that does not pass through the lived experience of the person himself is never capable of bringing about deep and lasting changes. The withdrawal of his projections from the outside world is a slow and gradual process, which I am able to facilitate only if at the beginning I accept the reality of the patient's paranoiac vision, letting him glimpse his projected psychic world only at intervals. James Hillman tells of a woman patient at the Burghölzli in Zurich who asserted one day that she had no heart.[88] A conventional psychiatrist urged her to put her hand on her chest to feel her own heartbeats, in this way denying her experience. Hillman insists that the patient's statement expressed a psychic reality and as such had its own validity. So if a man tells me that everybody hates him, I believe it since this is his psychic reality. Because we are dealing with a painful process, a good deal of time is required for the patient's paranoiac vision to give way to an interiorized perspective.

Indeed, the external object has the function of a scapegoat, and to single it out as the origin of one's misfortunes frees the individual from the unpleasant task of facing up to oneself. This is the basic criticism to be made of an exclusively reductive way of conducting an analysis: by looking only at the past and the relationship with the real parents, one runs the risk of never understanding that it is a question of an internal problem. An analysis conducted intelligently shifts our view instead onto the inner psychic world, but without eliminating the reality of the outside world: in this way the latter, deprived of our projections, finally comes to be seen objectively.

Thus the discourse I am developing should always be understood in an endopsychic sense, like the myths of which we are speaking. Returning to the psychic situation that Arion is presently going through, I confirm once more that the mythical metaphor we have used — the killling of the parents — has an intrapsychic meaning, and the discourses on the masculine and feminine aspects of the uroboric dragon should be read in the same sense.

Indeed, we have said that uroboric protection has two faces, the maternal and the paternal. To simplify matters, we might see in the heroic deed two distinct stages, the first of which, the killing of the mother, is the necessary condition for the passage to the next exploit. The feminine and maternal element must be confronted first, since, from the historical standpoint as well as the psychological, our first existential condition lies precisely in the "feminine," namely in the natural and instinctual world constituting the original base on which our psychic life and consciousness are structured. Unless we acquire dominion over this sphere to a certain extent, or at least a partial separation from it, life remains purely natural and therefore unconscious. Man, as a cultural animal, is born at the moment when he ends his total enslavement to the laws of nature, and this is possible if the will, understood in Jungian terms as energy at the disposal of consciousness,[89] is able to go beyond instinctual conditioning and point out new roads for man to travel.

All this is fully expressed in the first part of the Oedipus myth: Oedipus, in fact, kills the unconscious maternal element by solving the Sphinx's riddle, the answer to which is "man." There is, however, an interesting detail in this myth, which is that Oedipus, although he succeeds in accomplishing this first step, proceeds in his exploit in an unconscious manner: he kills his father and marries his mother without knowing it, and when he does realize it he blinds himself. His level of awareness is not such as to allow him to defeat the uroboric dragon completely. His act of self-blinding, which in Freudian terms is an upward transposition of genital castration, can signify his inability to assume responsibility for his own deeds and thus be the expression of a "spiritual self-castration," which is the renunciation of one's own being as a *subject*.

This aspect of the Oedipus myth introduces us to the problem of the killing of the father, the new task that Arion will have to perform if he is to proceed in his psychological development. We have seen the dream in which he was able to display his own genital organs without any fear or shame, and we have interpreted it as the overcoming of the fear of castration. This is equivalent on the structural plane to a consolidation of the ego and the "masculine," which has now assumed its autonomy in relation to the unconscious. Let us now see how a dream depicts the patient's present psychological situation:

> I see a small turkey and a female turkey pecking a large dead turkey, which they proceed to eat. I observe that this is normal behavior and wonder that books of natural history say nothing about cannibalism existing also among birds. It also occurs to me that the dead turkey is the father of the two little ones.

We learn from Arion's associations that the images in the dream have been aroused by a visit he had made a few days earlier to friends who live in the country and indeed raise chickens and turkeys. But from our standpoint, real events simply offer the material with which to compose a dynamic image that always refers to an inner development. He himself associates the young turkey with himself, and the female turkey with some "domesticated" feminine aspect of himself.

We think immediately of the woman who in a previous dream was watching him with admiration. But what strikes us particularly is the fact that these turkeys are eating the carcass of the *father*. The cannibal rite depicted in the dream seems to promise Arion the possibility of taking this essential step. Let us try then to understand what the "killing of the father" means on the psychological plane.

At the mythological level the victory over the maternal dragon is made possible by the help offered to the young hero by his "celestial father," and it is for this reason that "the slaying of the mother and identification with the father-god go together."[90] This means, psychologically, that once autonomy from the unconscious has been achieved, the ego falls inevitably under the sway of the "father," that is to say the actual governing principle on which the stability and continuity of consciousness are founded, they being in their turn the condition necessary for the creation of norms on which to base the life of the individual and of the group. As Neumann says:

> "The fathers" are the representatives of law and order, from the earliest taboos to the most modern juridical systems; they hand down the highest values of civilization.[91]

Despite this essential function — just as the protective function of the "mother" is essential in the first stages of existence—the "father," too, conceals fatal snares for the individual. Indeed, if a person's ego remains unconsciously identical with the collective norm that has been transmitted to it by education, it may totally dissolve in it and experience its own freedom of decision in only an illusory way. The individual thus remains inwardly dependent on a transpersonal authority that has already decided for him.

This dimension explains the moral inertia by which some people are incapable of seeing the injustice of the law, simply because the law by pure chance is on their side. Of course, there is no need to refer to major events in history, such as the Nuremberg Laws by which the Jews were considered an inferior race. It is necessary, however, to reflect on the fact that the Aryans did not protest in the face of the law's absurdity but hurled themselves like hyenas on the Jews, confiscating their property and depriving them of their professions: it was the *law* that allowed them to do it. One would think that these situations pertain only to the lower levels of society, but one should not delude oneself. The wild beasts protected by the law are to be found in all sectors. A classic example is offered by the physicist Lenard, Nobel Prize winner in 1905, who sought to demolish Einstein scientifically because he was a Jew.[92]

On the other hand, one must realize that the search for legal protection is in direct proportion to our ignorance. How many lives has the analyst seen devastated by doubts and devoted solely to the search for an external legitimization! Legitimization also accords with the desire of the general public, which sees in it a response to its own persecution anxieties. But for someone who is different? For him there is only the "killing of the father."

To kill the father thus means to strike down the prevailing order, that is, to gain awareness of the ways in which our acts are collectively conditioned, and to assume in the face of them a dialectical attitude that allows for individual solutions instead of collectively pre-established behavior. In this sense, the creative individual, the hero of the myth who subverts the status quo—which by its nature is always conservative—is the one who by his very development makes possible a transformation of culture, that is, the creation of a new vision of the world and of new values. What Neumann calls the "killing of the father" is therefore a fundamental stage, one that humanity has experienced countless times, as is shown by the changing course of history, but it is also an exploit that each of us must repeat in our individual existence, "for without the murder of the 'father' no development of consciousness and personality is possible."[93]

Here one might point out a fundamental difference in the way that the ego experiences the maternal and paternal principles. The first, for all the multiple faces with which it presents itself, remains essentially immutable; writes Neumann:

> For the ego and consciousness it [the mother image] always remains the world of the origin, the world of the unconscious. . . . It retains its unchangingness, for it is an embodiment of the everlasting and all-embracing, the healing, sustaining, loving, and saving principle.[94]

This means that our experience of the maternal continues to be influenced by a psychic structure that does not seem to be at all affected by time and is identically constellated at every moment of frustration, danger or dismay, whenever we feel the need to allay our suffering. The "mother" capable of giving us this beneficial milk is the same today as a million years ago; she is the instinctive assurance that frees us from every burden and every responsibility.

The father image, on the other hand, is much more tied to history and culture, that is, to a dimension of continual transformation. The paternal archetype therefore takes on specific connotations in various periods and cultures in relation to the canon of prevailing values. The confrontation with the personal father, as the bearer and representative of collective values, thus has great importance in the experience of the son, who often sees in him the true enemy with whom he has to fight. This then is the basic reason for generational conflicts, which are the expression of the infinite capacity for transformation inherent in the human condition. Indeed, where the transmission of traditions and collective knowledge takes place without shocks, being regulated by specific initiation rites during which boys are admitted to the society of adults, there is an implicit identification of the young with the standards handed down by previous generations. This makes any progress or change difficult, and the peace and stability of these societies are also indications of a cultural stasis and immobility. Their fate in antiquity was generally either violent extinction or else absorption by other cultures, which may have been ''barbarous'' in comparison to their victims but were certainly more mobile and vital.

Thus one can understand the mistake of so-called peaceful cultures that present a lack of conflict as though it were the highest fruit of democracy. Switzerland might be an example, as would any situation in which the transition from one generation to another seems to occur without disturbance. On the other hand, the argument applies to the personal level as well: if development within the individual is not accompanied by continual revolutions, we cannot speak of true growth. Instead we find ourselves faced with an expansion of premises that remain only promises, that is, unrealized potential.

For transformations to occur, it is necessary that the collectivity itself ponder — even if not in an explicit way — the possibility of a ''hero'' being born, an individual who, having acquired the traditional values of his culture, succeeds in evoking within himself what we might call images of the future, and in expressing them despite all the resistance put up by the collective. Here the clash between generations takes place, and it should not necessarily be seen in a negative light. At the concrete level, when we get along perfectly with our children and have an unruffled relationship with them, there is every reason to suspect that our rigidity and our fear of anything new are hindering our children from growing, and from expressing values different from our own.

Our fear may even be justified, since new things are not necessarily better than old ones. But in no case is it possible to grasp the meaning of the new message immediately, since the hero often anticipates future developments by centuries. Neumann is extremely clear on this point: the creative man is the one who is able to break the rules and enter immediately into a dialectical relationship with collective conditioning, expressed first by his personal father and then by society itself.[95] These are the persons who move history forward, ahead of their time by their ideas or their works, but paying a very high price on the personal level: silence and lack of understanding on the part of others.

Even without being "heroes" in this broader sense, each of us, to fulfill our human destiny, must enter into discussion with collective values, which with one's upbringing become part of one's own belief system, in order either to reject them or possibly even to accept them by a conscious choice. And then, even though we will not create anything new on the collective plane, we will at any rate have freed our individual existence from unconscious ties to a "law" formerly dictated from outside, by transforming it into an inner norm responsibly lived.

This, too, requires a sacrifice, and like every choice obliges us to abandon certainties and set out on the road of personal commitment and risk. Our attitude will in any case be personally authentic, whether or not it has general validity.

And so, to get back to Arion, against whom or what should he fight? What new message should he express? What cross must he bear? These questions are deliberately vague, in the sense that they can refer either to the individual dimension or the collective one. But whoever succeeds in traveling both roads at once — the struggle in the personal microcosm and that of the hero who overturns the world — knows that they are entirely analogous. The effort necessary is the same, in proportion to the strengths of the one who performs it.

The ambiguity of the questions stems from a fundamental condition of human life, which does not allow itself to be reduced to anything precise. And so the question about the very meaning of man is destined to remain forever unanswered. Hence the importance of the *riddle* as an archetypal foundation of life. In this connection, Colli remarks:

> A mystical condition is therefore presupposed, in which a certain experience turns out to be inexpressible: in this case a riddle is a manifesta-

tion in words of what is divine, hidden, and of an unutterable in-wardness.[96]

If the patient understands these things, the process goes forward since he is being introduced into a heroic dimension. Of course, we must keep in mind that every exploit carries its own risks and that momentary setbacks or waverings are inevitable. A month after the previous dream, Arion brings me this one:

> A house that stood on a sloping street has been blown up, and instead of the building there is a huge crater. It is full of rubble and even the beams have collapsed. I look at it without much emotion.

We might say that destruction has finally begun. Jung says that during analysis the patient is "like a rudderless ship."[97] A moment arrives when all reference points are lacking and the world seems to disintegrate. This moment, which generally coincides with a deep depression, is essential for the creation of a new attitude, a new way of observing one's own experiences. But it is also one of the crucial points of the analysis, teeming with risks, since the ego, which by now has lost the certainties of the past, truly finds itself at the mercy of a tempest. Considerable caution is therefore necessary, and above all much attention must be paid to messages that derive from the patient himself. The dream goes on as follows:

> I wonder whether I should go and look inside now that the cloud of dust raised by the collapse has dispersed, and see if there is anything left in the rubble that I could still make use of.

This dream tells me that we have surely destroyed old attitudes, but our friend is asking for a little respite: indeed, he feels the need to go back and see if something we have eliminated might not be re-covered. Faced with this dream, I realize that he needs to go more slowly. It was for this reason that in the next sessions I limited to the minimum any interpretation that might push him still further along.

The heroic life is characterized by the inner urge to continue on-ward to the conquest of the world. This last is to be understood, of course, in a very broad sense, which includes both the outer dimen-sion and the inner one. Thus there is in man a thrust, a dedication to the task of his own realization, that we might call "religious." Indeed, there are no rational explanations that can account for it. A physicist would smile at these words, but probably not a biologist, who, in order to understand the phenomena observed, is obliged to hypothesize an intrinsic finality in a process that seems to be determined solely by external causes.[98]

But the irresistible strength of this demand does not exclude in the course of the process the experience of fear, which, albeit not explicitly, has reappeared in Arion's last dream. His need to go back and look at residues of the past, the temporizing remark that derives from it, are basically the expression of a fear of the new, or in other words, of an attempt to go on clinging to a protective situation. This "regressive" tendency, always exemplified in myths, is the necessary counterpart to the individuated thrust present in man, which assumes a heroic character precisely because there are obstacles to be overcome, dangers to face.

Note that at the moment when the phase of the killing of the father is constellated, obstacles and fears also emerge in the patient to block the process, at least in appearance. Indeed, the myth tells us that it is the personal father — the embodiment of the old order — who imposes on one of his sons the task of confronting the dragon, with the secret hope of eliminating, by the son's death, the "new order" that would destroy him. In the context of the myth and in our human dimension, the one who is sent to fight monsters is always a person who is already suffering, discontented, depressed: he is a person who draws no life from the air he breathes in his surroundings because he grasps, if only at the emotional level, all their contradictions. He is, for example, the child who behind the superficially correct behavior of his parents is able to sense their unexpressed conflicts and the difficulties of their relationship. He will become a so-called neurotic, that is to say, the bearer of the family's hardships, and, at a broader level, those of the collective. It is specifically to him that the task of the heroic deed is given, in order that he be destroyed.

But if he is truly a hero, he preserves his critical spirit and his faith in the goal to be pursued even in his moments of fear; this allows him to defeat the dragon and to transform the same conservative forces that have driven him to confront it. This stuggle, which alludes to the continual conflict into which man has fallen, explains, according to Jung, why "Christianity rightly insists on sinfulness and original sin, with the obvious intent of opening up the abyss of universal opposition in every individual — at least from the outside."[99]

6

Creative Relationships

In the early days of analysis it was thought that therapy should be conducted in a state of "abstention," by which was meant the necessity of avoiding any vital decision during its development. This involves a total separation of the analytical dimension from real life, as though the two spheres — the inner and the outer — ought not in any way to interfere with each other. But through later experience the necessary interrelation between inner development and outer events was understood, and the reciprocal function of feedback recognized. This was something that Hegel had already expressed in *The Phenomenology of Mind*: "The force of mind is only as great as its expression: its depth only as deep as its power to expand and lose itself when spending and giving out its substance."[100]

Paraphrasing Hegel, one might say that man can be deep in two ways: *behind*, that is, with his eyes always turned to the past, or even to a hypothetical and never realized future, in which case he is completely paralyzed; or else *forward*, when he has the courage to bring his own thoughts and actions into the world and into the present, running the risk of making mistakes, but deriving even from these a meaning for his soul.

Very often patients — and the rest of us as well, in moments of difficulty — assume a paranoid and defensive attitude in the face of external reality, as though we found ourselves face to face with something that *really* has the power to destroy us, and that has in itself, as its essential qualities, connotations of good and evil. Instead reality is completely amorphous, and the power to mold it in such a way that it functions in relation to life lies solely in the hands of man.

It is precisely this possibility that is lacking in neurosis, thus placing us in a passive situation in the face of everything that happens. And it is our very passivity that gives to the world that malign appearance that frightens us so much, but which in itself does not exist at all except as a ghost of ourselves. And the ghosts continue to be projected onto the external world, there also to do us harm, if our understanding of ourselves remains confined within four walls and is not

74

translated into action, or in other words if it is restricted to the analytic field without being tested against real life.

The hero is the one who succeeds in taking this step, in looking the ghosts in the face, in order then to realize that they do not exist in concrete reality. But this is possible precisely by emerging from under the "paternal roof," expressing in reality one's own inner dimension, and discovering concretely that there exist other ideas, in relation to which one's own take shape. This alone grants the strength necessary to destroy the "father." This is why news is censored in certain countries: to know means to have strength; it thus means to have the capacity to oppose those in power.

In analytic therapy the moment of expression is thus extremely important, the moment in which the suffering person succeeds for the first time in operating in reality without carrying any projective and paralyzing baggage. At this point one's relationship with the "spiritual father" changes. This figure, who had only been imagined, and in the myth watches the hero's first steps impassively, now makes his voice heard within the individual and becomes an inner guide. Only now, after having demonstrated one's own capacity to face the world, is the hero truly such and truly the child of a higher father. Now his benevolence and protection are *deserved*. This dialogue with the "god within" is equivalent on the psychological plane to the possibility of reaching deep sources in our being, from which a new vision of the world can emerge. It is achieved, however, only if we succeed in deserving it by our actual deeds.

In order to convey how such a possibility might take place, it ought to be emphasized that at the beginning of the analysis the patient is inevitably prey to conflicting impulses. The libido is not concentrated, but dissipated like the water of a river into countless rivulets. As Leonardo said: "Just as every kingdom divided in itself is undone, so every talent divided into diverse studies becomes confused and weakened."[101]

Analysis (to keep to the metaphorical idiom) builds embankments and directs the river, with all its power, in a specific direction.

It should be clear, however, that when I speak of expression, I do not mean to favor an extroverted model of struggle, since the real creative confrontation always occurs on both fronts, outer and inner. Of course, there exist individual differences that ensure that some will embark on their heroic path in the inner dimension, while others will succeed in engaging themselves fully in the confrontation with external reality. But at a certain level of psychological development the two spheres tend to harmonize, out of a necessity for the development itself, which, were it to be arrested in one of the two positions, would be irrevocably stunted if not actually destructive. If my inner achievements, however profound, do not find a way to be expressed in the world, in my concrete and personal life, I remain a victim of the same ghosts that I thought I had unmasked, and am literally possessed by them. (W. H. Auden: "We are lived by Powers we pretend to understand.")[102]

Conversely, if all my achievements in the external world do not take on importance for my soul at a deep level, if they do not become significant psychic experiences, I have completely lost in them my subjectivity and the meaning of my acts.

This was the situation in which Arion found himself when he turned to analysis. His external success, stubbornly and steadfastly achieved, had lost any connection with his interiority, and therefore this man, although pursuing an artistic activity, felt alienated in work that set up no resonance within him. The blocking of his creativity, the symptom that drove him to seek help in analysis, was thus the involuntary arrest of an activity that had become an end in itself. A demand extraneous to his ego and to his will made itself felt through the imposition of a pause that allowed him to recover a dimension too long neglected. Without this dimension, the personality can only wither, like an old king whose exercise of power has become barren. Analytical psychology calls this "other" dimension with respect to the male ego the anima, and it appears in the myth as a female prisoner to be set free, a treasure to be discovered, the final prize in the hero's struggle.

In other words, at the moment when the individual truly succeeds in breaking his own unconscious adherence to whatever has determined his nature from both inside and out, it becomes possible for him to place himself in a creative and fertile rapport both with himself and with another person recognized as "other." Myths express all this in symbolic form, and as such suggest in a pregnant and significant way the ambiguity of these psychological experiences. That is why it is important for me as the therapist to succeed in activating in the patient an intuitive comprehension of the myth that he himself is living and that his dreams continue to express, in the same analogical form.

We have recognized an essential moment in Arion's psychological progress in the dream of the young turkeys that were consuming the remains of their father in a kind of ritual meal — namely, detachment from the values of the past in order to go forward and understand new things. Then we saw how the dreamer, again finding himself without any conscious orientation, felt the need to look back into the remains of a past that had become illusory. We worked together on this, and his subsequent dreams are evidence of the results:

> I dream of a plum tree, its fruit still green, but a few of them are ready to be picked.

This is a lovely image, full of significance for all its stark simplicity. The symbol of the tree is a familiar one: in the Biblical earthly paradise there is one with great importance for the destiny of man. And here too we have the same rhythm: some fruits can be picked, others not. I listen to this dream and experience it together with him, and we understand that now he can extend his hand and pick the ripe fruit, the fruit of the earth, of the unconscious. But there is something more, a sort of inner wisdom, of self-control, which suggests waiting and respecting the biological phases of ripening. In this sense, his need to linger over remains of the past is also illuminated but in a different way: from my discourse, which is also his, he grasps only what he is prepared to assimilate without harm and allows him to make gradual progress.

In the same night he dreams:

> I am on a very high grassy embankment, from which I want to descend but am unable to do so. Looking around, I see that just below there is a little street that ascends like a spiral staircase and would allow me to make a leap. Then I observe that a small leap would be enough to get off the embankment.

On awakening, he is calm, for he understands, and above all feels within himself, that it is possible to overcome the situation of paralysis. And, as the dream says, this happens by looking downward, where the feet are, where there is contact with the earth. In terms of analytical psychology, we might say that these dreams allude indirectly to an encounter with the anima (Jung: "the archetype of life itself")[103], offering the dreamer the prospect of a further deepening of awareness.

A month later, a female figure, whom we will call Thalia, appears in one of his dreams. She is a real woman known to Arion and destined to assume great importance both in his concrete life and on the symbolic plane:

Thalia has come to live temporarily opposite my old house, where I have returned. I would be able to see her from my window and be seen by her if the glass were not covered with ice that has accumulated during the winter. I start cleaning it, using a small scraper, while she smiles at me. But I'm not satisfied that we can only glimpse each other, and I go on working to clean the glass.

Such a dream could not have occurred at the beginning of the analysis, since it truly presupposes years of work. Before a man is able to establish contact with the deeper part of his personality, the anima, one must first come to terms with all the incrustations that not only make it hard to see external reality but in some way "freeze" our inner reality itself.

If we are not in rapport with the sphere of feelings and emotions — that is, if we do not make room in our conscious existence for an irrational dimension that in any case forms part of our being — then in some way this irrational dimension becomes a persecutory demon, or as Jung would say, an autonomous complex, which the ego is unable to manage and that can only be projected, like everything of which we are unconscious. This was the reason for the many mistakes in this man's love life. As I have already said, Arion's married life was unhappy, and as always happens, he blamed his partner for the failure. But with this dream we realize that what he lacked was the capacity to see into the world of the anima, that is, to live the experience of love in a transforming way. His own inner dimension, through not being aroused by a genuine human relationship, was embodied by projection in women who confirmed his unconscious negative expectations, thus becoming for him a scapegoat.

In the initial phases of analysis, the patient inevitably accuses others of his own wrongs and failures, and he does so all the more aggressively the further he is from awareness of the possible falsity of his position. Anyone who experiences a truth deeply, be it large or small, has no need to shout in order to affirm it. But the analyst must accept these paranoiac outbursts, which are particularly emotional when they involve the partner in a relationship, since the patient is not yet prepared to understand that his real enemy is himself. This, among other things, is the meaning of the mythological theme of the enemy twins, which can be constellated in analysis only after slow and patient work. The whole therapeutic effort consists in slowly removing the "ice" with the patient's help.

But why precisely ice? The dream image tells us that winter has just ended, a long period of lethargy during which this man has allowed useless things to accumulate. But now he understands that he must clean, because he is not content simply to glimpse. That he goes on scraping is a very encouraging sign, since it expresses the acquisition of patience, of a *religio* (scrupulousness), that one generally does not have at the beginning of an analysis. Indeed, patients always ask how long it will last, and obviously one cannot tell them, at *that* moment, that the development of consciousness is a process that will go on for the rest of their lives. But at this point the dreamer is not in a hurry, since he knows that in any case the fruits will not be lacking.

The fact that the process is virtually endless sometimes adds to the patient's doubts, while his basic assumptions encourage him to understand recovery the way it is considered in medicine. Apart from the fact that even in medicine the term recovery is, to say the least, ambiguous, it ought never to be used in depth psychology, since the process that Jung calls individuation — namely, becoming a totality that holds the contradictions of man within itself and dialectically arranges them — is actually unattainable. Individuation is a path, not a goal. The process goes on indefinitely because we always try to be content with wrong answers. But these unfortunately do not slake our thirst.

The last dream has thus seen the entrance into the analytic field of a female figure who will become very significant as the process develops. We have already said that the patient is married and does not have even a satisfactory, much less happy, relationship with his wife. Actually every relationship tends to slip toward unhappiness if the maturity of the two partners does not develop along parallel lines. The union that at a certain period in their lives allowed them both to satisfy certain given and generally complementary needs may turn out to be wholly inadequate upon the emergence of new requirements in one or the other. The collective conditioning that imposes the preservation of the relationship despite the personal hardships of the spouses, while having an undeniable social function, actually sanctions the unhappiness of human beings by condemning them to a relationship that, from the individual point of view, can only be regressive.

In the patient's experience, his relationship with his wife offers once again a mother-son dynamic that in the past probably satisfied his unconscious wish not to grow, and which pushed him into a protective dimension. This emotional choice also forms part of the same psychological picture that in the end brought him to neurosis and deep suffering, which, however, made dramatically perceptible to him the psychic death to which he had unconsciously pledged himself.

Let us now try to understand the meaning of the encounter with Thalia. For one thing, we can say that any significant encounter capable of activating new emotions in us, even if entirely accidental on the plane of reality, is psychologically made possible by a change in our inner condition, allowing us to grasp aspects of reality hitherto unseen. This means that at the moment of a new encounter something inside us is already prepared for this experience.

When a real person appears in dreams and the analyst asks the dreamer to describe him or her, it is in order to have information not about that person but about the patient himself, who, through his words, reveals his own experiences and his own way of relating to others. There is also the fact that in the analytic view, the dream, both as a total image and in its individual elements, always expresses a psychological situation of the dreamer.

It is in very positive terms that he talks to me about Thalia, this girl who smiles at him from the other side of the ice, terms he has never used in speaking of his wife. His description confirms the inner change that we have hypothesized by observing the dream image in its entirety.

We can say that the patient is no longer obsessed by the negative images of his parents, the struggle with the dragon has had a certain success and he is finally face to face with the "prisoner" to be liberated. What lies before him from now on is the task of achieving a new kind of relationship, with himself and with his partner. Now we can see more clearly how the dual aspect of the dragon was expressed in his incapacity to give free rein to his emotions and feelings, which always have a partially disintegrating effect on an ego that is still weak. Hence his need to live in reality a protective and "maternal" affective dimension, witl.out passion and without shocks, in a relationship that at the same time was accepted and sanctioned by the "father," that is, by the collective structure that stabilizes a priori the respective roles of the partners, while taking from them all freedom and all possibility of development.

Having unmasked and, at least for the moment, defeated the maternal and paternal aspects of the dragon, it is now possible to begin to glimpse the reality of a Thou and at the same time one's own, and thus to initiate a genuine dialogue with the *other* both within and outside us. In practice, it is a question of gradually withdrawing all those projections that are generally at the bottom of our emotional failures, and which keep us from recognizing the individuality of the person before our eyes while we continue our unconscious battle with parental images.

The confrontation with the anima for a man and the animus for a woman, which in the sphere of analytical psychology is considered an essential task for anyone who wants to, or rather must, set out on the road to individuation, starts precisely from this capacity to relinquish one's paranoiac vision of the world and of others. But once again it is necessary to recognize that what we consider an achievement is nothing but the point of departure for a new effort, one that requires the greatest commitment and is not free of dangers. To emerge from a protected and unconscious condition means to assume responsibilities, and in this particular case, to succeed in living a conscious relationship with an inner and outer partner, who is a real interlocutor and no longer a mother in whom to lose one's way or on the other hand an enemy to be fought. The danger is that of losing oneself again in the immediacy of what one is going through, of letting oneself be fascinated by the new experience, and thus not succeed in grasping on the subjective level, beyond one's emotional participation in the real experience, the psychological significance of what is happening.

And a dream promptly reveals to us the magnitude of the present dangers:

> I circulate in a hotel looking for a room where I know I must die. A thin man whom I don't know acts as my guide; his job is to explain things to me. I arrive at the door of a purple room with damask walls; I pause on the threshold and my guide tells me what is going to happen: I am to die from fumes of poison gas. Suddenly I wake up.

Although he doesn't enter the room in which he is supposed to die, I must still try to make him understand the "mortal" danger he is facing at this stage of the analysis. So I ask him for his associations to those poisonous fumes, and he tells me they must be incense, then he also thinks of a Turkish bath, and finally of a vagina. These associations, together with the obvious symbolism of the room, clearly refer to a maternal image, which, however, I do not care to interpret in an exclusively personal vein.

The "mother," understood in the broader sense as the unconscious, here appears endowed with a strong numinous quality and exercises a considerable attraction on consciousness. We might say that it is precisely the real and the dream encounters with the girl that have constellated a very deep psychic dimensioin which irresistibly attracts the patient. But the dream also tells us that at a certain level he perceives the danger inherent in a total surrender to the call of the depths. And since the patient himself associates the unknown guide with the analyst, we can posit that all this is the result of the analytic process, and that furthermore the security and solidarity that have been established in our relationship permit him also to see the risks he must face. To liberate the princess means to descend very close to the dragon, but without being swallowed by it. In other words, to recover and conquer one's inner reality, it is necessary to deepen one's contact with the unconscious, but without losing in it the quality of one's ego.

In our case, this process happens simultaneously on two levels, subjective (or endopsychic) and objective. This means that at the same time as a psychological advance is constellating a different female image within him, Arion meets a new woman in the outside world.

We have already mentioned our conviction that one cannot speak of simple coincidence. Basically one can say that we meet the "right" persons only when we deserve them, that is, when we are capable not only of making ourselves heard but also of being aware of those around us. For instance, it may happen that we feel a sudden interest in someone we have known for years, and this is generally due to an inner change that makes the relationship with that person significant. But once again the question arises as to how the endopsychic and objective levels interact. By saying that the confrontation with the anima is in any case an inner experience, one might imagine a psychological development that proceeds independently of our external reality. But on the contrary, experience shows that the two things go together, since the real stage on which psychological experiences unfold is always the concrete dimension of existence. The problem lies in grasping the meaning, the metaphor or the importance (in Whitehead's sense) that external events evoke within us. E. Bernhard wrote in 1947:

> Practical experience has taught us that it is precisely "external life," which in strictly Freudian analysis is reduced as much as possible so as to be absorbed into the transference to the analyst, . . . that brings us the help essential for the resolution of the neurosis, becoming, so to speak, itself a doctor and teacher. . . . The recognition that it has the same value as the material produced during the psychological pro-

cess requires that during the "treatment" external life also acquire a formative importance, at the same time that it asks to be formed.[104]

The Little Mermaid, in Hans Christian Andersen's fairytale, lives an unconscious dimension in the depths of the sea. Only at the sight of a prince, with whom she falls madly in love, does she begin a journey that will lead her to awareness. In order to win the prince and be able to live at his side, the Mermaid must face obstacles, but to go on living according to the laws of the sea, she must kill the prince. Because she loves him, she does not kill him. For this disobedience, she is transformed into sea foam, which by its nature is immortal. Now on the psychological plane, we can see how the path toward integration bursts out at the level of reality, that is, in the meeting with the prince. It will be later, after the assimilation of her own animus, that the Little Mermaid will be able to do without the love object. But note that here too, as in so many other fairytales and myths, the relation with the prince passes through vicissitudes, that is to say through a measuring of oneself against external reality that brings the inner psychological dimension into focus. The process is basically a circular one.

To be truly in accord with another person it is necessary to know one's own inner reality. For a relationship to be creative for both and be grounded on elements that cannot be dislodged, it is indispensable that each have conscious contact with his or her inner prompting of the opposite sex (anima or animus). Indeed, if I have established a working relationship with my feminine dimension and the woman has done likewise with the masculine side of herself, it is more difficult for there to be reciprocal projections of unconscious demands and expectations, which conceal themselves in both of us and make us live in the illusion of, and especially in the insistence on, a partner corresponding to our wishes. Stripped of our projections, each of us cannot be other than what he or she is, and a true relationship is based precisely on the acceptance of this reality necessarily different from our own.

More generally speaking, we can say that the external event is transformed into an authentic experience if we are able to grasp its inner significance. When we say that some people learn nothing from experience, this is because they never internalize the external fact, they never look for a personal meaning in what happens. Understanding the myth, especially in the sphere of therapy, can help us to change our attitude, because it allows us to recognize a broader, richer, more meaningful pattern in the apparent banality of our daily life.

A few days later, Arion brings me another significant dream:

> Thalia is wearing my hair, as though it were a wig. I can't see her face, but finally I see my hair from behind! It is very beautiful and curly, and I want to comb it, while being careful not to hurt her. Luckily the comb runs smoothly enough, almost without getting entangled.

The dynamic of projection is here very clearly revealed, and the dreamer, recognizing his hair on the girl, realizes how easy it is to dress the other in his own clothes. But in this way he also succeeds in seeing himself from an unusual standpoint (from behind), something impossible for a man by himself. This indicates with precision the need for human rapport in order to have self-knowledge,[105] and thus communicates to the dreamer all the cognitive value of the projection. And even though for the moment he does not see the girl's face, his concern not to hurt her is already a recognition of the other's reality, and of his own wish not to contaminate the relationship by projection. After a certain amount of analytic work, he finally understands that the negativity of a relationship is due less to the other than to himself. We will see later how statements of this kind should be taken with a certain caution, since a truly wicked and persecutory world can actually exist. I insist, however, as did Jung, that the withdrawal of projections is one of the fundamental points in the mysterious "curative factor."

It is common experience to realize how a certain intellectual laziness, combined with an inertia of the libido, makes us a-critical in the face of the world. We look at reality with an infinite number of prejudices, in general absorbed through the educational process. All this makes life easier in a certain sense, since we have no need to think but rather use stereotypes, which are often only a pale image of reality. Projection takes place particularly on human beings insofar as it is a function of our fear of confrontation. Through projection we see in others what we want to see and not what is really there. A relationship with another human being is always difficult because it does not happen immediately, but is built and developed in the light of the evidence and not of our presuppositions. In this sense, the true relationship takes account of human dignity. It is as though the patient, in the course of his psychological journey, had learned the value of his human dimension by entering into rapport with himself, and only at this moment is he ready to *recognize* the dignity of the other's existence.

On the other hand, one must also be aware that acceptance of the other seems to be one of the supreme goals of mature existence. This circumstance is unfortunately very rare, and furthermore it continually faces the analyst with heavy responsibilities. It may seem obvious that the analytical profession has as its fulcrum respect for the human person, but, as sometimes happens, when a principle becomes a working tool, it threatens to lose its specificity and dissolve in a formula that no longer has any relation to reality. The more the patient becomes aware of the other — that is, reduces his projections to a minimum — the more I am obliged to examine my own capacity for relationship, a capacity that years and years of work may have worn away, limiting it merely to a skillful professional style.

I must say that no analyst is ever sure of maintaining the dimension of human dignity appropriate to each individual patient. Something that might seem natural becomes, by a cruel joke, something to which the analyst must pay the closest attention. Thus the patient who makes progress on a human plane is a constant stimulus to the analyst's own development.

7

Death and Rebirth

If we examine the myth of the hero psychologically, we can see how in the successive phases a transformation takes place in the relationship between the masculine ego and the feminine element. From an ego originally contained and dissolved in feminine protectiveness (the uroboric situation), we progress through a passive dependence on the "benevolent mother" to a phase of violent opposition to the "terrible mother," culminating in the slaying of the dragon.

At this point a different kind of feminine element appears, one that no longer has maternal connotations and places itself as the partner of the male who has finally achieved maturity. And it is precisely the capacity to enter into a joint relationship with one's own inner feminine, which is always accompanied by the achievement of a genuine relationship with reality as well, that provides the possibility of entering into one's own creative values. Indeed, creativity is not based solely on the intelligence and the filter of the ego, nor, as some believe, on some autonomous productivity of the unconscious, but rather on a true interchange between the ego and one's own interiority. The difference between a work that is a simple product of the unconscious (or also, vice versa, a purely conscious elaboration) and the kind that is born instead of a true artist lies in the fact that the latter expresses at a symbolic level the profound relationship of the artist with himself, of the ego with the unconscious.

Arion is thus going through, in various ways, a highly important moment that may well prove to be a turning point in his existence. Another dream shows how he has changed:

> A tall thin fellow, more or less the same one as in the suicide hotel [whom he still associates with the analyst], accompanies me into a pharmacy and advises me to buy a medicine costing 48,000 lire. I try to have the price reduced, especially because from that moment on I will have to pay out of my own pocket and no longer through health insurance.

The medicine to be purchased is essentially his own recovery, but this is not something that an analyst — or anyone else — can give us, because, as the dream says, it depends on our strengths alone. Indeed, I would say that the medicine is precisely the energy that we employ in order to have it, that is, our awareness that we can no longer rely on some external group protection (health insurance) but must henceforth take the responsibility for it ourselves. The attempt to reduce the price also tells us that this acquisition can only be gradual: it happens with the progressive introjection of the meaning of the struggle against the castrating mother and the terrible father. From a psychological standpoint, to emerge from adolescence, and thus from the condition of being tied to the family and especially to the mother, means also to have the capacity to choose a suitable female companion, namely a woman who has the ability to respond to the new need for inner dialogue.

But the possibility of this encounter always depends on one's becoming aware of the inner elements that have hitherto directed one's choices. If this does not happen, one can find oneself in painful situations that in reality have little to do with the genuine pangs of love. When a relationship is born of an attraction that we are unable to account for in any way, of whose psychological meaning we have not the slightest idea, then as soon as passion is lacking all that remains is a sense of emptiness and futility, as though the pair had nothing to say to each other. To stay in this situation, even trying to justify it by an undefined feeling connected only with a long lifetime custom, means a kind of inner death for both. Indeed, if one does not live one's emotional readiness concretely and to the full, the sources of feeling dry up and with them the vitality of the inner dimension as well. Many neuroses are based precisely on this. The human being who does not touch his or her own depths, nor allow them to find expression in the outside world, is sick in the sense of being no longer a vital and creative person, but merely an automaton.

When we embark on an analysis in order to understand the reasons for our suffering, sooner or later we find ourselves faced with this problem and the unacceptibility of the psychic death to which we had been condemned. But at first, as we have already seen, it is on the face of the other that we see our death, and it is against him or her that we hurl ourselves. And in the same way, when a new need is born within us, it is inevitable that we look for its fulfillment outside. Indeed, to understand the inner roots of our existential choices does not at all mean to give them up, because in reality it is in "external life," as Bernhard has said, that we grasp our psychological dimension. And therefore one cannot claim to have made true psychological progress if one does not expand into real life, because in such a case one remains solely on a plane of intentions, without ever carrying them out. On the other hand, one should never forget that the analytical relation is able to transform the apparent disorder of suffering into a "path." Thus Nietzsche writes: "The anxiety of the soul . . . is perhaps the very condition that drives me to produce."[106]

In the sphere of analysis, one addresses oneself to the intentions, not to the reality, but the eyes of the patient and the analyst must always be attentive to how psychological development is diminished in reality itself. Here a particular point must be raised: reality, as has already been noted, can also be sick. For example, to go against the grain in a society of the Nazi type, in which insane and inflated statements were used to justify the atrocities that we all know, was an indication of psychological health and certainly not of illness. Allowing for obvious differences, each of us, proceeding gradually in our psychological development, must also learn to observe critically the world we are about to enter, and be capable of evaluating and distinguishing between our illness and the collective one. It is very important to understand this point because so much neurotic suffering is precisely the result of not having understood that what has gone wrong is not within the individual, but in the outside world.

Through acute suffering Arion has thus become aware of his own psychic death, and this has reopened the door to neglected inner dimensions, especially to that function of the anima that is linked to feeling and to relations with the other. This also means being able to make different choices in reality, choices that may correspond to changed requirements. Where one chooses blindly, for example in the case of a Don Juan, whether male or female, there is always repetition, that is, one always chooses the same persons because one is guided by an unconscious neurotic dimension, as automatic as instinct. When we succeed in penetrating our own inner reality, the coercive and obligatory nature of our impulses is broken and it becomes possible to make different, "freer" and therefore more satisfying choices. This continual reference to one's inner resources has a very precise purpose. And here I want to make it clear that in an analytic type of therapy the words by which one is saved are never imposed on the patient by the analyst.

Once again it is necessary to confirm the importance for human dignity contained in the treatment. As Jung states:

> We must first tread with the patient the path of his illness—the path of his mistake that sharpens his conflicts and increases his loneliness till

it becomes unbearable — hoping that from the psychic depths which cast up the powers of destruction the rescuing forces will also come.[107]

The patient has met Thalia, both inside and out, and at the same moment has felt more acutely the sadomasochism present in his relations with his wife. And these are moments when actual tragedies often happen, since generally one has not reached that psychological level that makes it possible to see things in a mature way. They are, however, "tragedies" that can lead to a salutary grasp of awareness and then, beyond the suffering they involve, they can provide the basis for further psychological development.

We have seen that in order to arrive at the encounter with the "prisoner," the hero must overcome difficult and dangerous trials, that is, he must fight the "dragon." The myths of all cultures, even those very remote from our own, describe this fundamental stage. Putting aside an often improbable cultural diffusion, we can go along with Jung in supposing that we are dealing with structural elements of the human spirit (archetypes), always identical even behind the multiple forms they actually assume in differing social and historical realities. This means that the exemplary models of man's relationship with himself and with the external world are expressed in myths, which is to say that when faced with typical situations man has typical ways of reacting. Whether he lives at the pole or the equator, if he is hungry he responds to this stimulus in the same way: by seeking food. But not only is our behavior influenced by the archetypal constellation active at that moment, but our very perception as well: if I am hungry, I appraise the world in terms of its edibility or not.

The typical image presented by the myth in the case of the hero is that of a sacrifice necessary for the conquest of the new; that is, transformation always occurs through a renunciation, a loss, a destruction. From Osiris who is reborn after being dismembered, to Christ who rises after his crucifixion, the basic theme is the same: death and rebirth.

The objection might be raised that to have recourse to myth constitutes an irrational response to the problems of life, and psychology thus could be accused, as indeed has happened, of not being scientific. But as Jung says:

> The intellect is the sovereign of the scientific realm. But it is another matter when science steps over into the realm of its practical application. . . . The intellect, and along with it science, is now placed at the service of a creative power and purpose. Yet this is still "psychology"

although no longer science; it is psychology in the wider meaning of the word, a psychological activity of a creative nature, in which creative fantasy is given prior place. Instead of using the term ''creative fantasy,'' it would be just as true to say that in practical psychology of this kind the leading role is given to *life* itself.[108]

And the fact is that life is not simply rational, whatever scientific minds may claim. The idea of death and rebirth is present everywhere, and so we can say that it constitutes a response by life itself to the problem of transformation.

When does a person begin to live? Science answers: at the moment of birth. But our psychological experience tells us that we truly begin to live when we emerge from a condition of being protected and begin to move independently, that is, when we leave the totality in which we are contained and accept the risk of death. In the animal kingdom, for example, the mother bear at a certain moment takes the cubs into the woods, makes them climb a tree and then goes away; it is the necessary weaning, like a second birth, which places the young bear in a situation where it must confront life alone. As for man, the protection he must give up is never of a biological nature, but psychological. We can say that our whole adolescence is a steady approach to the moment when we realize that our parents no longer count, that their words have no power over us. But to achieve this freedom, one invariably goes through many anxieties and fears, often badly concealed behind the characteristic adolescent rebellion.

This aggressive phase seems absolutely necessary for the independent structuring of the personality, so long as this attitude does not persist into adult life, continuing to disguise an ineradicable dependence. Youth, engaged in this struggle against the parents, is also expressed, as we have already said, in a typical idealism that harks back to absolute and transcendent values: this is the search for ''spiritual fathers,'' in which the young hero finds his own identity, different from the one offered by his personal father. Hence the emergence of new values and new ideals, which indicate to each individual the road he should take, a road that can also appear to lead back, but has validity in any case for the fact of being *his*.

The trials of life will later force us to verify our choices constantly and thus also to accept the possibility of further changes. Precisely in this flexibility lies the creative attitude of those who do not remain consistently faithful to a single view, whether derived from the personal father or from ''spiritual fathers.'' In other words, the development of which we speak is not accomplished once and for all at the end of adolescence, but arises every time that our way of seeing and being becomes absolute and threatens to harden our existence, under the aegis of a "father" whom we ourselves gradually construct for our own protection.

Much as individual situations of existence may vary, yet the model for the struggle we must conduct remains identical, depicted in the myths of all times. One of the functions of analysis is precisely that of making the patient understand the broader meaning of the conflicts in which he finds himself, whether his struggle lies in the professional area or in the emotional one. And since the analyst is typically the witness of several years of a person's life, and in some way becomes the interpreter of different moments that follow each other in time, he can recognize the stages that are gradually traversed and thus give the patient a key to interpretation that will also allow him in the future to impart a meaning to what happens to him. We have already said that the purpose of analysis is not so much to resolve problems as to teach a new way of placing oneself in relation to them, in order from time to time to find a solution that can only be an individual one.

Now, in the face of the patient's existential crisis — the collapse of certain situations that had hitherto seemed consolidated — and in the face of his depression, it is extremely important to make him understand the great archetypal motif of death and rebirth. As many myths suggest, every possibility of transformation passes through what is called "dismemberment," experienced for instance as confusion or extreme disorientation, as when for the first time we say no to our parents but do not yet know what we should do. If we are able to endure this lack of reference points, which is always a harsh and painful experience, we embark on a phase of apprenticeship during which we learn to construct our own compass.

It is a period of intense suffering, but one that constitutes a fundamental transition that we cannot avoid, on pain of rigidity and psychic death. It is here that old acquisitions dissolve and possibilities for a new direction are simultaneously created: life germinates at the very moment when the seed opens and is in a certain sense destroyed. Writes Jung: "It is as though, at the climax of the illness, the destructive powers were converted into healing forces."[109]

Within this same framework lies a certain way of conceiving the acute schizophrenic episode and its fanciful deliriums, that is, not as a psychological breakdown but rather as an autonomous attempt at readjusting the personality. In cases of this kind, basically similar to neurotic disorientation although admittedly much more serious, it is essential that the patient perceive a presence capable of receiving, and in this way "containing," the spread of fantasy. This listening attitude makes it possible to insert the products of the schizophrenic's imagination, following a serious crisis, into a significant framework since they become *real* communication in a relationship with another person ready and able to understand them. Experiments in this field have shown how this kind of treatment involves considerably fewer relapses compared to drug therapy, which is virtually limited to blocking psychotic manifestations, and with them the possibilities for a reconstruction of the personality.[110]

Returning to Arion, it is clear that he must now examine himself in relation to a partner on whom he has for years projected his difficulties. By now he has understood the unconscious dynamics that have bound him to his wife, and he has established a relationship with another woman. How should he behave in the presence of his wife? It is surely a situation of conflict, and therefore a painful and extremely difficult moment, because one must also reckon with the emotional reaction of the other, who is not always ready to be told certain things. As Bernhard says:

> When in a psychological confrontation, one of the two life companions does not wish to cooperate, then a separation is essentially foreshadowed and tries to take place. If the one who solicits this confrontation does not succeed in separating, he or she becomes ill and may thus create a situation that apparently stamps him or her as the negative part . . . of the partnership, while the other vaunts his or her rigid attitude as firmness, equilibrum, and "normality." Doubtless the first loses his equilibrium, but from the standpoint of development, he or she is the more alive, the richer, the one who goes forward, and therefore the one who is worth more.[111]

There is the danger at these moments of receiving unnecessary blows, of punishing oneself for one's own need for change, and therefore of not succeeding in taking the crucial steps. On the other hand, it is also possible that the inner drive to change may be experienced *only* on the level of outer reality, and therefore in an aggressive manner in the presence of the other, who is actually seen as the enemy to be destroyed. In this case, too, no transformation within the individual occurs, since the total projection of his own ills onto the other does not permit him to become aware of his own personal responsibilities, and reveals a failure to internalize the matter.

One of Arion's dreams is particularly eloquent about his way of experiencing and confronting the situation:

> It is night, and my wife goes home with me after having prepared me a meal. It would seem to be my home, but I'm not sure. Anyway it is on an upper floor and is illuminated by the moon. I then think of myself as a "pimp," like a film director who tries to create a certain atmosphere with a moonlit night. There is a note of gentleness and melancholy, both in me and in my wife, and at the moment of parting she tells me with simplicity and intensity that she still loves me. I reply that I still love her too, kiss her quickly on the lips, and leave. I awaken with the feeling that I have had a good dream.

Certainly the dream can be seen as the manifestation of a wish, the wish for something that in reality he does not have, but I think it much more productive to interpret the dream image as the expression of a *possibility*. Furthermore, as Kierkegaard reminds us, the wish is a symptom not of an outer lack but of an inner richness.[112]

If dreams are, as Jung says, "self-representations of the psychic life-process,"[113] this one tells us that the patient now has the possibility of experiencing in a mature fashion the separation from a dimension that by now has been overcome; and "in a mature fashion" means specifically without aggression and without emotional involvement. The gentleness and melancholy that shine from the dream reveal in any case that the experience is not being scornfully thrown away, but that its psychological meaning is being heard and understood.

Another interesting feature is the emphasis placed on the moon, a female symbol par excellence: the dreamer is illuminated by one of his own deep dimensions, that creative femininity that he has encountered within himself and with which he is beginning to carry on a dialogue.

As I have said several times, it is an illusion to think that analysis can transform the external world — for this purpose we must use other instruments — or that it eliminates the conflicts borne by the patient. Actually what is transformed by analysis is our way of seeing things, within and outside ourselves; that is, it changes our relationship with ourselves and with the world that surrounds us.

Men have always had a tendency to reason in terms of their immediate experience. For example, seeing the sun rise and set, people thought for thousands of years that the sun moved in space and the

earth stood still. The naive mind believes what the senses tell it: un-
mistakably the sun rises and sets. It took an enormous critical capacity to be able to state and then demonstrate the opposite of this evidence,
and we also know at what price.

The same is true of psychological life: it takes a great deal of effort
to make us understand that reality is not exactly as it appears to our
subjective experience. At a more general level, we can say that the
true progress of consciousness is not so much due to the discovery of
something new, or to the simple accumulation of data, as to, in Jung's
words, "criticism of the psychological assumptions upon which a
man's theories are based." And he adds: "The investigator needs a
lot more facts which would *throw a light on the nature of the psyche*," because only by being aware of our manner of looking can we
hope to have a somewhat more objective perception of reality.[114]

And thus it is in analytical experience: to become aware of unconscious contents means to strip others of our projections, that is, to
realize what lenses are altering our vision. It is therefore not the external world that changes, but our inner dimension. The last dream
we examined is evidence of it: by the light of the moon the dreamer
sees his wife in a different way because *he has changed*. There is no
longer aggressiveness, but recognition and acceptance of the other.
This involves the acquisition of a certain emotional distance and thus
also a differentiation from the other, of the kind that makes it possible to transform aggressiveness into an affectionate "I love you,"
uttered at the very moment of separation.

Aggressiveness basically seems to be the primary mode of relation
with the external world, and we can see it not only in children at play
but already in newborn infants. Sucking, crying and demanding the
mother's presence are aggressive acts that permit survival; but if in
the course of development one does not become aware of this model,
which we might call archetypal, and which determines us from within,
any situation in life can become the occasion to exercise one's de-
structiveness. And the more people are emotionally involved, as in a
love relationship, the more they run the risk of mutually annihilating
each other, sometimes using subtle psychological means and disguis-
ing their aggressiveness behind the facade of a supposedly boundless
love.[115]

Some maintain that frustration is *the* cause of aggressiveness in the
presence of another, and this is true especially when an excessive
dose of frustration is suffered at an early age, that is to say by a psy-
chobiological organism that is still extremely plastic and sensitive to

environmental imprinting. But excessive or unjustified frustration is merely one of the expressions of an authoritarian structure of relations, which lies equally at the root of two opposite neurotic conditions: that of a person whose attitude is predominantly aggressive and transgressing, and of one who lives in a state of passive dependence and is utterly incapable of self-assertion. These two modes, which are regularly encountered in analysis, are perfectly complementary and mirror to the same degree the individual's fundamental lack of differentiation. In other words, aggressiveness and passivity in relation to another reflect the relation with one's inner world, the relation between consciousness and the unconscious; they are therefore both signs of a "civil war" within the personality, of which the individual has not the slightest awareness.

Analysis, which proposes to establish harmonious relations between the ego and the unconscious, specifically involves breaking up this aggressiveness-passivity model, which we might also call authority-dependence, in order to achieve peaceful cooperation among the various demands of the personality. And the first step on this path, which is often long and difficult, is precisely to become aware of those aspects of our inner conflict that we project onto the outside world. Only at this point is it possible to witness the "miracle" of a person who, after having hated the other for years, or been his or her passive victim, begins to be creative, since he recovers all the energy he had hitherto employed in attacking the other or defending himself.

On the mythical level, after having faced dangers of every kind and slain the dragon, the hero comes into possession of the treasure. And here a new problem arises, one that precisely concerns the use of this "treasure." In dynamic terms, once the neurotic knots are untied, there is the problem of how to channel the energy that has been made available. Analytical psychology does not at this point offer ready-made answers, particularly ones valid for everyone, nor does it speak of a more or less automatic "sublimation" of childish impulses. Instead it proposes a continual search for individual solutions, which can be of the most diverse kind, as diverse as people themselves. Nevertheless, in accordance with Jung's theory of archetypes, it is possible to recognize three basic models to which man's different ways of utilizing his "treasure" can be traced.

One type of hero is the extrovert, whose aim, writes Erich Neumann, is "action: he is the founder, leader, and liberator whose deeds change the face of the world."[116] He is the man who sees external difficulties and social problems without being paralyzed by them; he seeks concrete solutions, expanding his role in the world and using his strength and intelligence in an effort to transform reality.

The introverted hero, on the other hand, is the one who seeks to introduce the values of inwardness into the world: Socrates who offers a new vision of the world, as does Buddha or Christ. These are persons who discover within themselves a truth, a value, and make an effort to communicate it. Extroverts, then, confront the dragon on the outside, in the reality that surrounds them, and it is there that they fight their battles; while introverts perform their exploits in the world of ideas — they are the ones who fight and kill the dragon of collective values.

The third type of hero is of particular interest because he is closely related to the discourse of analysis. Indeed, this type "does not seek to change the world through his struggle with inside or outside, but to transform the personality."[117]

To know and transform themselves is the task of those individuals who personally experience the dialectic between nature and culture, unconscious and consciousness, inner world and outer world, without choosing either of the two poles:

> In this sense, the growth of individuality and its development are mankind's answer to the "perils of the soul" that threaten from within, and to the "perils of the world" that threaten from without.[118]

This is the model of psychological creativity, which seems to be carried out in the most complete silence, but finds expression in every aspect and at every moment of individual existence. In the presence of this type of person, the distinction between introversion and extroversion no longer has any value, since what takes on importance is an intermediate dimension, which from the Jungian standpoint is the only reality immediately given to man: *psychic reality*, where inner and outer come together in the very *meaning* of individual existence.[119] The value protected and elevated in this view is precisely the individual, as a subject responsible for his own choices, who consciously places himself at the center of a conflict inherent to man himself (collective consciousness and the collective unconscious):

> The ego keeps its integrity only if it does not identify with one of the opposites, and if it understands how to hold the balance between them. This is possible only if it remains conscious of both at once.[120]

This is the goal of *centroversion*, the constitution of a stable point within the personality, capable of becoming aware of the dual fascination emanating from the outside world (collective values) and from the unconscious world (primordial images).

By pursuing a linear and adaptive development, the ego gradually comes to govern the personality and enacts a similar role in the world, but behind its selfish goals and illusory freedom there is an uncritical adherence to collective standards and a total dependence on the outside world. The fascination of power is almost irresistible for most people, who do not realize that they are paying for their presumed accomplishments with their own psychological slavery. We know that Jesus, before beginning to preach his message of transformation, had to resist the temptation of the devil, who offered him the possibility of becoming the ruler of the world. This means that in order to express something new, it is necessary to come to terms with one's wish to dominate the world and then take the proper distance from this desire.

The condition of schizophrenia, on the other hand, can give us an image, albeit an extreme one, of the opposite risk, that of succumbing to the inner forces, to the numinous aura of the unconscious. This means letting oneself be directed by inner messages, without any attachment to reality, and it also means to lose control over one's life. It is one of the dangers, which Jung never underestimated, of contact with the unconscious, as a result of which the ego may be dissolved unless it is able to preserve its capacity for critical thought.

In both cases, man loses any possibility of change, since the individual nucleus that ought to perform the transformation remains identical with one of the poles (the outside world or the unconscious), and therefore can only perpetuate a schism that is actually a one-sided condition. The significance of the individuation of which Jung speaks, a process by which man becomes *individual*, differentiating himself from what determines him, lies precisely in his capacity to transform himself continually by mediating in his own oneness the conflict between the inner and outer worlds. The results of this mediation can only be individual, and when we refer to particular expression in myth it is not to seek answers to the problems of man, but to grasp the *structure* of the transformation process, which seems to be identical in every human being. Knowing the myth, we can understand the patient's suffering and place it within a broader framework, whereby it acquires the significance of a preparatory moment for possible transformations. As Jung says, "The merely reasonable, practical attitude of the rationalist, however desirable it may be in other respects, ignores *the real meaning of suffering*."[121]

The myth of Osiris, for example, is especially rich in elements, found also in the Christian tradition, that are capable of illustrating the exemplary model of transformation, which always passes through a ritual death, a sacrifice, followed by a rebirth. We can say that every patient, at the time when overwhelmed by suffering he presents himself for analysis, is in a situation of death, and his neurosis lies precisely in his incapacity to see its transformative value and to find the path of rebirth.

The artist of whom we are speaking here was a destroyed person, blocked in his creativity, and in his relations with his wife he was living his aggressiveness toward his own feminine dimension. By accepting his own suffering and sinking into the depths of his unconscious — and this also means agreeing to live consciously his own psychic death — he was able to discover within himself a different feminine dimension and to free himself from the aggressiveness that, although projected on the outside world, was directed primarily against himself. Here then is another dream, expressing even more explicitly the change that took place in Arion, a change we have already grasped, albeit as only a possibility, in the previous one:

> I am walking along the Tiber and remember that this is a place where I have always seen construction work in progress. I look at the river astonished and amazed: I have never seen it so beautiful, green and flowing, but also so placid in its descent to the sea. The water is clear and luminous, there is no longer any trace of construction work, and where before there had been a crumbling embankment, there is now an almost geometric architecture of evergreen hedges. Likewise at the point where there had been rapids, the water has been curbed and flows smoothly thanks to a small dam, it too clothed in greenery and standing out against the water in a wealth of colors.

The construction work, the crumbling embankment and the rapids are all expressions of an unsettled existence devoid of meaning, subject to influences and disturbances coming from all sides. The river, which is a beautiful metaphor for the flow of life and psychic energy, now moves in an orderly manner thanks to the work of man, who is able to build dams when necessary. This is to say that the transformative work of the conscious individual intervenes to impart a different direction to the forces of the unconscious.

A dream like this can allow us to proceed in the analysis with a certain confidence, since it indicates that the words that have been spoken between us have not been thrown to the winds, but have taken their place as part of a profound experience.

8

Immense Light

In the Egyptian myth of Osiris, the god, having been killed and chopped to pieces, is reconstituted by Isis, his sister and bride. But one part of his body, the phallus, cannot be found, and Isis replaces it with a wooden one. And it is with this wooden phallus that the dead Osiris impregnates Isis, who gives birth to their son Horus. This impregnation with an artificial organ is one of the essential elements of the myth, just as in dreams the strangest aspect is often one that expresses something particularly significant. We can see in it a fecundity no longer merely physical and material, but actually *spiritual*. The creativity that follows the dismemberment is thus of a spiritual nature, as in initiatory rites all over the world, such as in the Christian tradition, where the Holy Spirit is the heir of Christ.

But in the development of mankind and in that of every individual, this mythical image encounters considerable obstacles, since man is led to believe by his historical and social conditioning that he must carry out his actions solely in the material world, the master of which he must in some way become. That is to say, we are encouraged to think that the confirmation of our existence as men depends upon the real possession of things: thus power over others, wealth, or in Jungian terms the "persona," become the essence of life itself. But the more that man, in the course of his development, consolidates his material dominion over the world, identifying it as the meaning of his life, the more he loses the capacity for spiritual creation. This is one of the profound reasons why some religious orders, and not only Christian ones, place such emphasis on the idea of poverty: to be deprived of all earthly goods means to relate to the world by trusting only in one's own spiritual strength. "It is not Poverty," says Rilke, "but the immense Light that shines over the soul."[122]

Failure to acquire and possess the things of the world is often the apparent cause of much of the suffering we encounter in analysis. Possession of the world means among other things a successful marriage, a certain course of studies, a certain kind of job. And for many people a reasonable solution in these areas of existence can mean the cure of the neurosis. For others, however, suffering is truly

99

alleviated only by an inner development that leads to a different vision of life and the world: what is necessary for them is the kind of psychotherapy that aims at *transformation*.[123]

It is not, of course, something that can be imposed, since as Jung points out, "the needs and necessities of mankind are manifold. What sets one man free is another man's prison."[124] For the need for transformation to emerge it is necessary to experience first-hand how useless the possession of things can be and to discover directly that adaptation to the demands of the world is not always sufficient to satisfy the needs of the soul.

Very often the objective difficulties presented by reality are seen as the single cause of our failures, but this paranoid vision keeps us from looking inward to seek the deeper meaning of our distress. Of course, it cannot be denied that many aspects of the world are indeed cruel, and can have an adverse effect on our psychological equilibrium and our chances for concrete achievement. But this happens because the laws of survival, biological and social, take no heed of individuals, but only of the species or of society. Totalitarian systems, for example, have no regard for the existence of the individual, since they consider only large groups, and it is this that in practice hinders their functioning; indeed, individuals do not perceive the meaning of social transformations, but only the limits imposed on their own freedom.

Psychological maturity, however, makes it possible to see the cruelty of the world as an objective fact, in the same way that physical ailments are objective. Sickness and social injustice can in part be eliminated, but it is utopian to try to imagine a kind of human society that would not have certain negative aspects from the standpoint of the individual. On the basis of the concepts of Melanie Klein, we can hypothesize the presence of an inner persecutor, which originally manifests during nursing in the relation with the mother's breast. This dimension is never completely eliminated, and it is always ready to be projected onto the outside world. The real obstacles that arise to frustrate the fulfillment of our wishes activate the inner persecutor, and from this suffering is born. For example, if a thousand persons participate in a competition for a single job opening, this objective fact is experienced at the personal level as an aggressive act. The suffering that derives from feeling oneself excluded and from perceiving others as enemies is one of the strongest that can be felt, since it evokes that early experience lived in relation to the full or empty breast of the mother. An external and objective difficulty becomes subjective suffering: I am being persecuted.

Unless we succeed in transforming our view of things, it will always be external events, be they good or bad, that control and determine our lives. A young man once asked Einstein what he should do to protect himself from the suffering that the world inevitably inflicted on him. Einstein replied that he should imagine himself living in a world of Martians and not of humans, and thus avoid any involvement with what was going on around him.[125]

To succeed in understanding that the world doesn't "have it in for us," but is simply what it is — even if sometimes terrible, as when a natural catastrophe occurs — means to emerge from an undifferentiated psychological condition, similar to that of the child and the primitive, in which a distinct subject does not yet exist but only the group, which is also at one with the environment. Differentiation is necessary in order to acquire an individual consciousness, able to observe external events with a certain detachment and to decide responsibly how to confront them. But broad as our awareness may be, there always remains in us an emotional sphere that participates in the collective dimension and in some way undergoes its influence. And this raises the question of manipulation, always possible when, consciously or not, the strings of emotion are touched, inducing in the other person a regression in which all personal responsibility is lost. Manipulators of consciousness exploit precisely this possibility of regression and contagion, which inevitably spreads in a group when emotionality emerges in even one of its members.

The same danger exists in analysis, since the continuation in the patient of an emotional sphere untouched by consciousness makes him susceptible to the slightest manipulation, even involuntary, on the part of the analyst. Hence the need for the analyst to be wholly aware of this unconscious game and of his moral responsibility with regard to the person in his presence. It is a subtle game, since the patient risks never growing up and not wanting to face reality. It is as though he felt the benevolent and paternal surveillance of the analyst. As Machiavelli said, "Men, when they are well governed, neither seek nor desire more freedom."[126]

Thus I must continually question myself on the validity of my interpretations, asking myself here, for instance, if the psychological advances attested by Arion's dreams are really the fruit of a deep maturing process on his part and not simply the passive assumption of a view of the world that pertains to me. And this applies particularly to an important dream like the last one we have seen, in which a dam gave a new direction to the river of life. So it is necessary to examine carefully what is happening in the patient's real existence and compare this with the dream messages. Let us look at the next dream:

> A carpenter who has been in my house is about to leave. I reproach him and tell him that there is still something in the kitchen that needs to be fixed. The carpenter replies that he has already fixed it and I myself will be able to make any final adjustments that may be necessary.

In the carpenter it is easy to recognize the figure of the analyst, and the interesting fact is that he is being dismissed. That is to say, the process of separation is beginning, although the patient in some way is resisting it. Here the possibility of manipulation arises, but the dream tells us that he himself is capable of carrying on the work that remains to be done. The dream continues:

> At a certain point I see a coal stove that I didn't know I had. But the carpenter tells me I had merely forgotten about it, he has found it hidden away in a closet.

The dream, in its symbolic language, alludes to a transformative instrument (the stove) that has always belonged to Arion and which he must now consciously take possession of. To think that the analyst can perform transformations in us is still a residue of that emotional sphere that does not accept personal responsibility and nourishes itself on the influences of others. But the dream offers other interesting aspects:

> As he is leaving, the carpenter suggests that I take a look at some closed rooms. I ask whom they belong to, and the carpenter, laughing, replies that they are my own. Then he leaves. I turn to look at the door, repeating to myself, "other rooms, other rooms." Then I awaken.

This is certainly a dream that can only be had toward the end of an analysis, since it reveals to the patient that what he has derived from the analytic relationship is not so much a particular knowledge of himself, but rather a way of entering into contact with his own inner dimension, and thus also the awareness that his own possibility for transformation arises through individual solutions to the problems that may periodically present themselves. As the dream implies, the investigation of oneself is never completed once and for all, but engages one's entire existence; the closed rooms, which still form part of Arion's house, clearly indicate this further possibility for development, which Arion will have to carry out on his own, without relying on the analyst for what at this point would only be manipulation. In other words, the risk of manipulation is reduced in direct proportion to the patient's ability to continue working on himself alone, opening ever new doors, and not only on the dream level.

This dream, in which there appear new rooms to be opened and explored, clearly alludes to the possibility of broadening or enlarging the personality. This is a problem in which man has been interested since earliest times, while having recourse to the most varied techniques in order to deal with it. Plato well expresses the human need for a broader awareness, which is always linked to a condition different from the pure rationality of the ego, when he declares in the *Phaedrus* that "the greatest boons come to us through madness, which is granted as a divine gift."[127] All over the Greek world "madness is the matrix of wisdom."[128] But this profound psychological truth can be completely distorted, as, for example, in the modern use of drugs that in some way alter the normal condition of man. These substances, such as LSD, have the power to carry a person into a dimension undoubtedly broader than the consciousness of the ego, but what is generally not taken into account is that if the ego does not participate in the "trip," the expansion of consciousness thus obtained is only ephemeral, when it is not actually harmful. That is to say, people overlook what Plato took care to stress: the profound difference between the insanity of the "mantic, possessed, delirious man" and the wisdom of one who instead "judges, reflects, reasons, solves riddles, and imparts a meaning to visions."[129]

The transformation and broadening of the personality that occur through analysis presuppose a continual confrontation between the ego and the unconscious, in which both poles are modified precisely because the ego understands what is happening. "Confrontation," writes Elie Humbert, "is the difficult art of accepting the strength of the other without losing one's own."[130] It is just this need for conscious vigilance that rules out the use of drugs, which owe their effects to a dissolution of the ego; as Jung says: "In the final analysis the decisive factor is always consciousness, which can understand the manifestations of the unconscious and take up a position toward them."[131]

The dream thus urges Arion to deepen further his relation with the unconscious, which he must personally and responsibly confront, with all the dangers that this entails. And his next dream expands on this theme:

> I go down to inspect the cellar. There are large holes in the walls like electrical current outlets. Streams of water flow from some of them, and water also oozes from the walls. My attention is drawn to one of these holes, which has an attachment into which one might screw an electric bulb. Then I see a shower of sparks and realize that there is dampness and electricity everywhere; the very atmosphere seems to be crisscrossed by electric charges.

The theme of depth is obvious: the cellar represents what is underneath, the unconscious, the dark place of repression or of what has yet to be expressed. But the dampness oozing from the walls gives us a sense of the difficulties the ego must face, that is, the possibility of being submerged by unconscious forces. We have previously seen some very forward-looking dreams, offering a resolution; how then should we interpret this disturbing image, which seems to bring back a danger that we thought had passed?

I think this dream is communicating a very important message to the patient, namely that the unconscious always retains a strong force of attraction for the conscious mind, and that whatever progress we may make in our psychological development, it does not take much to return to an instinctual level. The instinctual level, in man's case, does not mean only biological impulses, but includes thoughtless adherence to unconscious convictions and opinions, thus rendering actions automatic. The psychic sphere, as compared to the instinctual, is characterized precisely by the capacity for reflection,[132] which places a filter, a delay, between the stimulus and the response. The neurotic person does not act consciously on the basis of reflection, but reacts in an immediate way to outer stimuli.

In the course of an analysis, the patient and I must never delude ourselves about having reached "maturity," since at the very moment of being so convinced, we would have lost it again. This is the tragic aspect of man's existence, and at the same time his greatness: the possibility, which for some becomes a necessity, of constantly transcending and thus overcoming one's nature. On this score, Freud was quite right, declaring that analysis certainly does not make people better and that analysts are not necessarily better than other people. Analysis offers only a tool for understanding, one that allows us to enter into contact with our contradictions without claiming to eliminate them once and for all.

And it is indeed a contradiction, a profound ambiguity, that Arion encounters in his dream, at the moment when he is deepening his relation to himself. In the cellar he finds water and electricity, two elements in themselves opposed, which can fecundate and illuminate, or on the other hand inundate and destroy. It is the typical duplicity of the unconscious, and as Jung says, "The insinuations of the anima, the mouthpiece of the unconscious, can utterly destroy a man,"[133] unless he is capable of facing them and consciously choosing what to do. In other words, the positive or negative valence of our inner images always depends on the attitude of the ego and its relations with them.

But there is still an essential step to be taken, which is to see how the contradiction expressed by the inner images is reflected in real existence, and then to bring back into it any understanding that one is able to have of the unconscious. We already know the patient's contradictions: he is a public person who is afraid to expose himself, a man who while wanting to love does not know how to do so; we have seen the enormous gulf that lies between his external position and his inner sense of incompleteness and impotence. When one has such a feeling, one justifies everything that happens in reality, good or bad, without ever taking a position in relation to it; but the moment one begins to be aware of one's own strengths, one also acquires the courage to face the dual reality, inner and outer, that in some way determines us, and above all one learns to tell them apart. At this point in the analytic process, Arion is emerging from such a discovery and must struggle against the inertia of the unconscious, which makes him conservative in spite of himself.

This tendency toward the preservation, which means also the repetition, of the past is typically childish, but it is something that accompanies us throughout our lives, because it underlies a need for security that is never completely fulfilled. Children, for example, enjoy having the same stories read to them over and over again; they do not want the slightest variation. As adults, too, we all have fixed habits, almost rituals, which indicate the degree of our insecurity. The authentic and desirable human condition, however, is the one in which, fear notwithstanding, one agrees to the change that by now has become necessary. Thus in every analysis, a moment comes when one must take decisive steps, and generally one must overcome a strong resistance, precisely due to that psychic inertia that tends to keep things the way they are. It is essential not to miss the right opportunity, since it may be a long time before it offers itself again.

The act of courage that one succeeds in performing once, apart from its specific value, becomes a highly important acquisition for the future as well, since it introduces the person to a dynamic process in which he will more easily be able to accept further, albeit painful, transformations.

Arion has understood for some time that he ought to leave his wife, with whom no further dialogue is possible; but, as we have already noted, it is a very difficult decision since he must fight on two levels, the personal and the collective. He has realized that his inner gains have no meaning unless they are confirmed in real life as well, but at this point fear re-emerges, the same fear that the child feels in being separated from its mother for the first time.

Underneath this fear, inextricably bound up with a sense of guilt, we can discern the problem of the relation between the individual and the collective, a problem that invariably turns up in the course of our existence, albeit at different levels. I have seen many human lives destroyed through the inability to take a personal stand in relation to the collective. The collective, whether internal or external, has fixed rules in accordance with its general interests, which do not take account of individual demands. And so our singularity can find room in the world only if we succeed in recognizing what our genuine needs are, and on that basis finding the courage to break collective rules, especially those we carry unconsciously within ourselves, constituting the so-called superego, or in Jungian terms the persona. Courage is needed to support and overcome the inevitable feelings of guilt, which are reinforced by the reaction of the collective itself. In the past people went to the stake for asserting a truth that conflicted with the law of the collective, but even today loyalty to some spiritual value of our own carries a high psychological price.

At the level of the couple as well, we find the conflict between an inner law pointing to an individual path and the collective law forbidding the breaking of an oath. But the very rigidity of the collective rules governing the life of the married couple reveals the intrinsic fragility of the situation, that is, the ever present possibility that the individual will make independent and different choices.

Faced with the need to break a familiar structure, by now nonexistent on the psychological plane, Arion is afraid and his ego totters: in the dream we see water and electric sparks. There is also, however, an electric outlet into which a bulb could be screwed; that is, it is possible to have light.

The unconscious seems to be indicating to the patient the necessity of truly living his conflict, since only in this way will he be able to clarify and understand his psychological situation. And at these moments the anlayst cannot help re-assessing the extent to which he himself has been ready to compare his own individual law to the collective one, and to which of the two he has adhered. Indeed, the distinctive feature of analysis lies precisely in the fact that if the analyst has not traveled a similar road, clarifying it to himself, the patient too will remain confused, or worse, might be driven to do something that the analyst has not succeeded in doing, thus repeating a dynamic very often present in the relations between parents and children, where the children are delegated to live the unconscious demands of the parents.

In the analytic process, it is not so much words and interpretations that have an effect on the person, but rather, as Jung points out, the psychological essence of the interlocutors:

> Hence the personalities of the doctor and patient are often infinitely more important for the outcome of the treatment than what the doctor says and thinks. . . .
> The doctor is therefore faced with the same task which he wants his patient to face.[134]

And so it is only if I have lived and relive with the patient the conflict between individual and collective values that I can help him to understand that at certain moments it is necessary to make a choice.

I recall that the session ended at this point. It was a day in November, and he understood, with beads of sweat on his brow, that he could no longer turn back. Though experiencing fears and uncertainties, Arion knew he would have to leave the house in which he had lived with his wife, thus putting into effect what he had learned on the psychological plane.

It must be emphasized here that to recognize one's own projections, to become aware of the unconscious dynamics by which we have lived in reality and in our relations with other, and to perceive within oneself new needs — all this does not mean ipso facto having to demolish certain external situations, nor that this is the only possible solution. As we have already said, the real change is always essentially an inner one, involving a new way of seeing things, and especially an emotional detachment that allows us to face reality without being crushed by it. The classic example is offered by the relation-

ship with one's parents: to emerge from the condition of childish
dependence, it may not be necessary *literally* to leave home, but one
must learn to carry on an adult dialogue, stripping ourselves and our
parents of the inner images of which we are all bearers, and which,
as long as they remain unconscious, perpetuate a mutual interdepen-
dence. By changing we can induce a restructuring of the overall situation and thereby a corresponding change in the persons around us as
well. At this point it is possible to make a conscious and responsible
choice, which can even be to stay.

But, as we have already said, reality can be sick, that is to say, the
persons with whom we must deal may not be ready for change nor
prepared to accept a new dimension in the relationship. In such a
case, to go on clashing with them or giving in to their demands can
only be regressive, and their neuroses reflect and perpetuate our own.
In any case, one should keep in mind that the choice between accepting a certain reality or destroying it is always up to the individual,
and from the analyst's standpoint what counts is not so much the
reality in itself, but the way in which the patient relates to it. But one
should also add that an analysis in which psychological gains are not
accompanied by *any* external change, however small, is basically
suspect, since the field of experimentation of the unconscious is always
consciousness, namely our everyday life.

Arion and I now find ourselves in a final phase of the process, at
least that part of which I have been a witness. Indeed analysis never
arrives at definitive conclusions, since these depend on the actual life
of the patient, who at a certain moment must leave the analyst and
put to use the tools he or she has acquired.

9

Conscious Discrimination

Let us now try to sum up in psychological terms the mechanisms that allow the development of individual consciousness, a development that we have followed through one patient's dream images and through mythological amplifications. As I have mentioned several times, this is a process that is continually repeated during the whole course of our existence, always at different levels: consciousness is a boon that has to be continually re-acquired, and this alone constitutes our psychological redemption.

One of the first fundamental transitions is what Erich Neumann calls the "fragmentation of archetypes": "The breakdown of the amorphous unconscious into the picture world of archetypes enables them to be represented and perceived by the conscious mind."[135]

It is a rupture of the original ambivalence, of the emotional bond with the collective whereby every distinction is annulled. This fragmentation makes isolated qualities perceptible, splits unity into pairs of opposites, and allows consciousness to exercise its functions of discrimination, evaluation and choice of a direction. Consciousness, to be able to know the world, needs to divide it up. We can see an example in scientific research: the greatest advances in knowledge are due to a fracturing of the object of study. This method, which can even be called reductionist, makes it possible to go forward, since we cannot grasp anything from the totality. In order truly to understand something, we are obliged to concentrate our attention on a single aspect of the whole.

For example, in the relation with the feminine, fragmentation of the archetype allows one to approach it by differentiating the terrible aspect from the positive one. When this happens, a man can free himself from his unconscious fear in relation to women and truly come to know their creative sides. Arion, too, had experienced this mixture of good and bad, this deep emotional ambivalence that stifled him in the presence of women. Analysis allowed him to separate the two aspects and thus to begin a cognitive process. Let us look at a dream of his that is highly significant in this respect:

In unfamiliar surroundings, like the waiting room of an airport, I am

109

seated at the table facing an unknown young woman. I speak to her and tell her: "You're very beautiful." The girl moves her lips, as though to emit sounds, but nothing is heard; then, as though I had learned to transform sounds into words, I hear her say: "I think we'll do things together when we get out of here."

On the psychological plane, beauty refers not to the outward appearance of the other person, but to profound harmony that is established between the two. The airport suggests a temporary situation, a trial situation most likely aiming precisely at this encounter: we can recognize in this image a metaphor for the analysis that is coming to an end. But another important element that merits consideration is that at first the dreamer does not perceive any response. It is the problem of communication, of man's solitude, which can be considered structural; indeed, at a certain level, there is nothing more to say to the other person. But it is also true that every process of development is in some way the acquisition of a capacity for communication. Initially, then, the patient does not hear and does not understand; he sees only lips that move. This represents his difficulty in relating to the interiority of the anima, basically the real problem that brought him to analysis in the first place. But at the moment of communication he also perceives the possibility of moving out of a temporary dimension: Arion and the woman in the dream will leave the airport — the analysis — and do things together, since real contact with the unconscious has begun.

Of course, this "doing something together" has only a marginal application to the sexual sphere and alludes essentially to a creative potential. It also has to do with a basic question often raised by the patient, namely the possibility of his ever living a true relationship. The problem of anyone who has never had a human relationship, or has had only mistaken ones based on projection, is that at the moment when he is faced with the genuine possibility of a relationship he does not live it to the full, always fearing it will founder. This means that past experiences have the power to condition us in the present as well, but this is true only if we do not become aware of what determines us.

There is yet another important element in the dream: the patient and the woman are facing each other, and this "face-to-face" attitude is characteristic of the human being, the only one of all living species capable of observing something by making use of interpretative categories, that is, having a view of the world of which it is possible to be aware. The dreamer observes the woman before him, expresses an evaluation (a feeling judgment), and this allows him to know his own value system, his "metapsychology."

Here I am moved to make a more general statement, which also concerns the problem of orthodoxies. When suffering drives us to question ourselves, a first level of response can be found on the philosophical or religious plane, that is, in already existing systems that offer quick and ready answers to man's problems. These are therefore collective answers, and can never fully satisfy the individual, who carries with him his whole experience of life and his unique and unrepeatable psychological complexity. Whoever stops at this point inevitably becomes a dogmatic person, obliged to defend rigorously the principles to which he adheres and the answers in which he believes, without realizing that his rigidity and unbending orthodoxy conceal doubts that his conscious mind is obviously unable to tolerate.

On the other hand, whoever succeeds in sustaining the tension of uncertainty will keep up the search for answers, which at this point will be only personal; and if he also succeeds in making them conscious, they may become a new philosophy or a new metapsychology. Jung, for example, lingered for a while over Freudian concepts, but after a period of some confusion succeeded in expressing his independent thought and creating his own *Weltanschauung* or view of the world. It is a serious matter when one is apparently speaking in accordance with certain categories, while in reality expressing others of which one is totally unaware: one can thus speak the words of Christ but be profoundly atheist — which means that beyond our conscious intentions there are unconscious responses to our suffering that in fact control our life itself and our relations with others.

All those who are interested in psychology have found some answers that have satisfied them. I personally have felt a particular resonance in the formulations and attitudes of Jung, while other colleagues may have found it in the message of Freud or of other writers. But we would all be dishonest, with ourselves and with those who seek our midwifery, if we did not take note of the fact that Jung or Freud are of relative value, and that we in any case have gone on and express a view of the world that can only be called our own. What counts is the awareness of our personal standpoint, on the basis of which we act in life, since this is the operative factor and not whether we are Jungians or Freudians. In other words, it is essential to overcome the emotional relation — which is also identification — with the so-called school to which one belongs. Indeed, a school can be an alibi or a resistance against seeing what we are, without labels or medals.

The fragmentation of archetypes goes along with a progressive weakening of the unconscious, which also allows some control of its emotional components. The "deflation of the unconscious" is the result of a process of elaboration and rationalization through which, in Neumann's words, "the symbol is broken down into conscious contents, it loses its compulsive effect, its compelling significance, and becomes poorer in libido."[136]

That is to say, the unconscious loses part of its strength, which is then employed to broaden consciousness. This view of Neumann's comes close to the now classic formulation of Freud: "Where id was, ego shall be." In other words, while the psyche of the child or primitive reacts in an almost reflex fashion to the pervasive action of the unconscious and the disruptive emotional charge of its symbols, a more evolved consciousness is able to separate the material content from the emotional component and thus to appropriate for itself partial aspects of experience, which in this way become the object of knowledge. The reaction then becomes freer and more considered with respect to the emotional determinants. The primitive condition is equivalent to having petroleum without knowing it: it is then possible for it to gush out suddenly and flood the surface. If instead one is able to convey it through the proper equipment, carefully controlling the output, such richness is in part utilized.

It is therefore necessary to channel the forces of the unconscious through the medium of consciousness, and this also happens by means of a devaluation of emotionality and of everything that is not perfectly clear and perceptible. In the primitive condition, there is the risk of being swamped by the unconscious; the development of consciousness includes the opposite danger of shutting off the source of emotion for good. Psychological vitality lies instead in the possibility of finding a middle way that allows one to excavate within oneself and to make one's inner riches flow out by conscious activity. In any case, it is essential, especially in the first phases of development, to succeed in neutralizing the emotional components, since they interfere with cognitive processes, that is, with differentiation.

This is a phenomenon that we all know. For example, when we go to take an examination, if we are overcome by emotion we are no longer capable of using the cognitive system, which means that our consciousness is no longer able to listen and respond adequately. The capacity to hold the emotions at bay and to use them or not depending on the situation forms part of normal psychological development. The integrated person is precisely one who can keep a certain distance from emotionality when it is necessary to act on the basis of conscious directives. The failure of certain political splinter groups dominated by emotion is particularly a result of this incapacity to make the right decisions at the proper moment. Without knowing it, they are in reality therapeutic groups, but they fail even in this purpose because they lack a conscious center of reference.

The fragmentation of archetypes and the neutralization of emotional components, which produce a weakening of the unconscious and a strengthening of the sphere of the ego, also have as a consequence what Neuman calls "secondary personalization":

> There is a persistent tendency in man to take primary and transpersonal contents as secondary and personal, and to reduce them to personal factors. . . . The personal psychic sphere peculiar to the ego emerges from the torrent of transpersonal and collective events.
>
> Secondary personalization is also connected with the process of introjection and the interiorization of "outside" contents.[137]

This tendency progressively reduces the power of the unconscious collective dimension and correspondingly increases the value of the individual personality. The divinities and numinous powers that formerly lived outside are now interiorized and come to form the foundation of the individual. But their archetypal roots, which remain unconscious, continue to be projected outside onto persons of the real world, and this provokes "a necessary but exceedingly dangerous confusion of the person with the archetype."[138] This phenomenon, an example of which is offered by Jung in "The Relations between the Ego and the Unconscious,"[139] happens very often in the course of therapy, where the analyst becomes the bearer of "divine" images that actually pertain to the deepest sphere of the patient. Any intensely emotional situation can give rise to projections of this kind, as commonly happens in experiences of love.

In the development process of consciousness and the ego, according to Neumann, a further differentiation of the faculty of "abstraction" also occurs:

> Thus the line runs from primitive man's total possession by the primordial images to a final situation in which deflation of the uncon-

scious is so far advanced that the idea is regarded as a conscious content to which one can . . . take up an attitude. Instead of being possessed by an archetype, we now "have an idea" or, better still, "pursue an idea."[140]

The undifferentiated emotionality of the archetypal experience thus becomes detachment and knowledge: man actively places himself before the world and feels himself to be an achiever.

Arion thus felt overwhelmed at first by what he produced, and did not recognize himself in his performance. He was submerged also in his emotional relations, and for this reason was obliged to retreat. His last dream reveals to us how the capacity for abstraction allows him to place himself in the presence of the other, and thus also in the presence of himself: he is starting to become the master of his own life.

I would not want to give the impression that it is easy to follow the progress of an analysis simply by analyzing dreams. Anyone with therapeutic experience knows that things develop differently and that each encounter is isolated from the previous ones and from those that will come later. Only with the passage of time is it possible to make connections and recognize a continuity that at the time is not always perceived. In the course of therapy many other elements contribute, along with dreams, to give a sense of the path on which we are traveling, and by no means the least important is the kind of *feeling* that is established in the relationship with the patient, which also varies depending on the amount of time spent together. Signs on the nonverbal plane are moreover accompanied by remarks concerning the field of awareness, that is, the sphere of reality, which always constitutes the experimental terrain on which psychological gains occur.

We have seen that in the last dream Arion, face to face with a young woman, told her she was beautiful. We have also stressed that such a statement has a psychological meaning only if it emerges from the perception of the other in her totality and in the dimension of a relationship. Thus the feminine image reminds us not only of an outer reality but of an inner one, the one we have called the anima, and with which the hero must make contact in order to fulfill his destiny.

At this moment, after he has begun a dialogue with his anima and has succeeded in leaving behind the childish situation represented by has relationship with his wife, Arion brings me another very significant dream:

I am having a discussion with a builder about how to make my house more spacious, without extending it in width or height. The builder leads me to a square trap door measuring about three meters on each side. Looking down into the opening, about three meters deep, I expect to get dizzy. I lean slightly forward and see that the steps are narrower than the length of my foot, and are thus impractical. But I am surprised to discover that I have no feeling of dizziness or fear. The bottom is neither dark nor threatening, and so I think of going down by putting my feet slantwise on the steps.

We can immediately make associations with previous dreams in which a feeling of dizziness and the fear of falling appeared, but the particularly interesting thing here is that at this point in his psychological journey Arion realizes that further development of his psychic "house" is to take place below the surface, in the inner depths. That is to say, we have arrived at the moment when it is necessary to question the very values of the ego in relation to a totality that transcends it.

From the psychological standpoint our lives can be divided into two parts, in which completely different needs manifest themselves. In the first, survival itself has a prime value, and everything that one does has a certain narcissistic connotation. The newborn infant is the prototype of this narcissistic condition, from which there gradually develops an organization of the libido oriented toward the object. Youth is thus a progressive expansion of the world, contemporaneous with a broadening and consolidation of the sphere of the ego. The patriarchal culture in which we live reinforces this mode of existence to the point of considering it exclusive and predominant, to the serious detriment of the totality of the individual. Indeed, to live only in terms of the ego and its needs means to have been conditioned by collective values that offer only external — hence fleeting and superficial — goals. But the very drama of life, which not everyone is able to perceive, can lead eventually to the realization that two dimensions exist, one of concrete possessions, wealth and power—precisely that of the ego — and a dimension rather more "spiritual," which does not seem to be affected by real acquisitions, nor even interested in them. Hence Jung says in his autobiography:

The more a man lays stress on false possessions, and the less sensitivity he has for what is essential, the less satisfying is his life. . . . In the final analysis, we count for something only because of the essential we embody, and if we do not embody that, life is wasted.[141]

It is very hard to succeed in understanding what is "essential" and no one can teach it to another, since it is always individual. This is the task of the so-called second half of life, to find a balance between the demands of the ego and what is required by the actual totality of man. What then is the problem of our artist Arion, and what is the nature of my problem in relation to him?

We are always looking in two directions: outward at what is taking place in the world, and inward. Dreams allow this twofold vision since they show simultaneously how the individual relates to the internal and external. The analyst in particular must pay attention to both dimensions, keeping in mind the possible lure of the external, which seems to give an immediate reply to our expectations. This explains, for example, why Max Weber's theory on the Protestant ethic and the birth of capitalism seems so convincing.[142] He maintains that capitalism was able to succeed in Protestant countries especially because in their view of the world social achievement is in direct proportion to God's love for man.

The dimension of the ego and outer reality is extremely alluring, and not only for the patient. Many analyses are conducted solely on this level, even though psychological concepts of the unconscious are used. But in this way they neglect the reality of the anima, which represents what lies more deeply within us. The anima is expressed through contrasexual figures and is all the more repressed the more our adherence to collective values, which want us to be totally male if we are men, forces on us a one-dimensional existence, and does violence to our psychological totality. This one-sidedness, obtained at the expense of the contrasexual demands, ensures that the relationship between man and woman will be based exclusively on reciprocal projections. And this means not to have any authentic relationship.

Arion has taken a path that has allowed him to see the infantilism of the ego and its one-sidedness, and thus to emerge from a condition of maternal protection, on which a self-centered and narcissistic ego nourishes itself. Now he is ready to enter into a true confrontation with his own interiority and with another person, and to establish an I-Thou relationship (Martin Buber) in which each partner has an independent existence. The meeting with a real person, the girl we have called Thalia, took place at the same time as this inner development by which he passed from a way of life founded on the ego and on outer success to one that requires a constant relationship with the unconscious. The richness of the inner life relativizes the importance of external success, which does not always correspond to man's real needs. As I have mentioned, the difficulty lies in the fact that no one can know a priori what is essential for him: the hero always finds himself having to choose among different paths the one most suited to his inner psychological dimension.

The anxieties and dissatisfactions of life derive precisely from the fact that we try to satisfy the demands of the ego, without realizing that this is impossible since the ego is like a miser who is never content with what he possesses.

When he comes into analysis, the patient's eyes are invariably turned toward the things that are not going well in his concrete reality: if his love life is unhappy, it is there that he looks, or it may be to the sphere of work. But even if a miracle were to resolve the external problems, the dissatisfaction that derives from a life lived only on the plane of the ego would by no means be eliminated. For existence to have a meaning, and suffering as well, it is necessary to understand what Arion's dream points out — that our truest growth does not occur through an extension in "width" or " height" but in depth. And depth means being able to grasp the symbolic message that even the crudest reality has to convey to us; it means establishing our identity as human beings on the continuum of meanings that are no longer ephemeral like those of the ego, which make it the passive victim of external events. For this reason, I always respond with symbolic language to anyone who is ailing and speaks to me in concrete terms. With the passage of time this juxtaposition can have transforming effects on the other, who thus learns not to respond directly to his own demands, and to question himself instead about their symbolic meaning.

Here a very important problem arises, since none of us can say with certainty what it is that acts in a transformative manner on the patient. On the other hand, similar phenomena occur also in the field of medicine: aspirin, for example, is unquestionably a painkiller and an antipyretic, but no one knows exactly how it works.

It is undeniable that the analytic relationship sometimes leads to radical transformation. Although the actual therapeutic factor is unknown, the crucial characteristic of the analytic encounter may be that one person raises questions about himself in front of another *who knows what to listen for*. There can certainly be some psychological development through a process of introspection conducted in solitude, so-called self-analysis, but only in the presence of another who has been there oneself is it possible to approach other points of view and truly to see other paths. Recognition of the analyst as an interlocutor different from oneself, and the attention of the analyst to what is expressed in the patient independently of his ego, allow contact to be made little by little with a psychic reality with which the ego is not identical and which has much deeper roots. It can at least be said that Arion, in the course of a long dialogue with himself that took place in my presence, came to understand that his suffering was due to a lack of rapport with his anima, his inner woman, and to the consequent hardening of the ego that amounts, as we have already said, to a psychic death. As Jung describes it:

> Only when all crutches and props are broken, and no cover from the rear offers even the slightest hope of security, does it become possible for us to experience an archetype that up till then had lain hidden behind the meaningful nonsense played out by the anima. This is the *archetype of meaning*, just as the anima is the *archetype of life itself.*[143]

For years Arion and I questioned ourselves about his suffering, which inevitably touched my personal suffering and forced me to re-examine my own convictions. Together we were able to understand that to evaluate existence only in terms of the ego leads to a blind alley since the ego is always dissatisfied. With his last dream the patient makes a new discovery: he no longer feels the dizziness that had blocked him in the past; he can look beneath the surface and above all can descend in an individual way. Indeed, he cannot use those stairs in the traditional manner, and only for a moment is he gripped by fear. His attitude has profoundly changed in that he now finds a way of descending that is consistent with the situation and at the same time individual.

10

Human Dignity

Man is thus faced with two essential tasks during the span of his existence, tasks apparently opposed but aiming toward the identical goal of fulfilling his individual destiny. We can assign them schematically to a first and second half of life, but without giving any specific time period to these two phases, which are only of a psychological nature.

The first half is characterized by the need for a differentiation from the unconscious matrix, the indistinct uroboros from which the individual psyche gradually emerges. What encourages the formation of a conscious center of the personality, the ego, is called by Neumann the tendency toward *centroversion*, "the innate tendency of a whole to create unity within its parts and to synthesize their differences in unified systems."[144]

The development of the ego from an undifferentiated matrix, for which we can use Neumann's term *original self*, happens in a completely unconscious way; this means that the ego is unaware of its dependence on a totality that acts as a formative guiding principle, analogous to the one that at the biological level maintains the organism in a state of equilibrium by coordinating the activities of the various organs.

The task that we perform in an almost automatic way in the first half of life is thus the structuring of a personality centered in the ego, and able to act in the world in accordance with conscious directives for the purpose of guaranteeing the biological and psychological survival of the individual. But this development, as we have seen on the mythical plane as well, involves a selective differentiation of some functions and the repression of others. It involves, that is, a clear separation of the conscious and unconscious systems, and hence also the risk of an excessive one-sidedness of consciousness, which may lose all ties with that totality of which it is a part. The differentiation of the ego, indispensable to the development of civilization, is also a loss of the original plenitude. In Jung's words:

> The breakdown of the harmonious cooperation of psychic forces in instinctive life is like an ever open and never healing wound . . . because the differentiation of one function among several inevitably

leads to the hypertrophy of the one and the neglect and atrophy of the others.[145]

The education we received in the family or at school tends from the beginning to develop one particular function — thinking, feeling, intuition or sensation, according to the Jungian model — since singleness of direction and specialization always go along with greater effectiveness. But, as Jung says, "The privileged position of the superior function is as detrimental to the individual as it is valuable to society."[146]

Indeed, society can pursue its goals only on condition that each of us acts in a determined direction, knowing how to do certain things in the best way and not others. This means undoubted progress on the collective plane, but also a renunciation by the individual of not only potential skills but also aspects of his or her personality. If, for example, I identify myself exclusively with the rational sphere, and also succeed in conceiving elaborate theoretical systems that go to increase the common cultural heritage, I pay a very high price at the personal level with the repression of feeling, or of other fundamental dimensions that ought to nourish my existence.

The task of the second half of life is the harmonization at a higher level of the various parts of the personality; it is the conscious realization of the tendency toward centroversion of which the ego is no longer the passive object but the conscious protagonist. The extreme differentiation of consciousness, with the deep split that it creates within man, is also the means for beginning that search for totality which according to Jung characterizes the process of individuation.

To return to Arion, let us recall that he came to me driven by suffering, since his worldly success had not been accompanied by a sense of inner richness, but rather by a feeling of emptiness and dissatisfaction. In the course of the analysis, we both saw that his success had been achieved at the expense of that inner dimension Jung calls the anima and which represents a most thorny problem in a culture like ours based on the masculine and patriarchal values of consciousness. Societies of this kind require a radical polarization of masculine and feminine characteristics, forcing individuals of both sexes to repress all the contrasexual aspects that are nevertheless part of their nature. This phenomenon leads to dissatisfaction and also to aggressiveness, especially on the collective plane. Indeed, repression of the contrasexual renders destructive the energy that, if used consciously, would be a source of creativity. And it is a fact that societies that do not assign men and women opposite and well-defined roles, on the basis of "pure" masculinity and feminity, are much less aggressive.

From childhood on, we in the West experience this educational tendency aiming at the clear polarization of masculine and feminine, and there are painful moments when we feel, if only unconsciously, as though we were losing something of our inner richness: in school, for example, when the teacher calls only on the intellectual faculty of the pupils, completely ignoring imagination and feeling. Or else, as commonly happens, when only extroverted ways are encouraged and the behavior of introverted children is considered almost pathological. This is true violence done by the human being to oneself, and the result is a more or less total repression of imaginative activity. There seems to be no place in our culture for fantasy, which Jung calls "the clearest expression of the specific activity of the psyche":

> The relation of the individual to his fantasy is very largely conditioned by his relation to the unconscious in general, and this in turn is conditioned in particular by the spirit of the age. According to the degree of rationalism that prevails, the individual will be more disposed or less to have dealings with the unconscious and its products.[147]

In a culture like ours, based on the values of the ego and on adjustment to external reality, fantasy is by and large unacceptable; it is like a child's game that must be overcome in the name of a reality and a seriousness that are actually only sclerosis. But again as Jung says,

> We know that every good idea and all creative work are the offspring of the imagination, and have their source in what one is pleased to call infantile fantasy. Not the artist alone, but every creative individual whatsoever owes all that is greatest in his life to fantasy.[148]

In short, we can say that we are brought up for the purpose of achieving maximum efficiency in a specific function, like a worker who specializes in a particular job. But the person so one-directional, and thus so efficient, loses his psychological depth. One might offer an equation: the higher the degree of efficiency, the more does existence come to lack breadth and depth.

This is the inevitable effect of a line of patriarchal ego development, whose watchword, "Away from the unconscious, away from the mother," sanctions, writes Newmann, "all the devices of devaluation, suppression, and repression in order to exclude from its orbit contents potentially dangerous to consciousness."[149]

In the analytical journey described here we have encountered these problems, with all the bleeding wounds that had brought this man to external success but also to the loss of his inner guide. His energy flowed only to the outside: he could paint pictures and even sell them, but every painting was a drop of blood lost forever.

In a certain sense one can see the analytic relationship as a possibility of stopping this rush toward "efficiency" — toward the one-sidedness of the ego — and reflecting on those aspects of ourselves that we have renounced. This is the task of the "second half" of life, a second half that can begin at any moment since it corresponds to the profoundly individual need. Jung said that persons marked by destiny can be recognized early, and his personal history is a testimony to it. The difficulties that some already as infants encounter in nursing, something that should be absolutely natural, are an indication, according to Jung, of that *dira necessitas* that obliges some to seek from the beginning their own individual mode of existence.[150] Many people who come to analysis must become aware precisely of this irresistible drive toward their own fulfillment, which does not allow them to adhere to received collective responses, at the cost of a condition of incurable conflict with themselves. It is this wound that many carry into analysis, thinking at first that it ought to be healed and eliminated. As we have already, said, the whole educational system is directed toward the transmission of received knowledge and the condemnation of any hint of deviation. We know very well the feeling of humiliation when we are accused of not understanding something, when in reality we understand it better than others. It is an example that recurs throughout life, and it is necessary to realize that the obstacles we encounter do not demonstrate our incapacity but the need for a broader understanding.

What happens in analysis is the exact opposite of what happens in life: the true meaning lies in what had appeared to be nonsense and what was considered an error is revealed to be full of significance. But above all we learn not to fear the world, for as Rilke says in his *Letters to a Young Poet*: "Has it terrors, they are *our* terrors; has it abysses, these abysses belong to us; are dangers at hand, we must try to love them."[151]

By the end of a thorough analysis, an actual reversal of viewpoint often takes place, clearly revealed in dreams. I recall, for example, the last dream of my analysis in America: "I had to go and buy some flowers and I entered a shop by the seashore. I bought the flowers and took them to someone." My original condition might have been described as involving a one-sided differentiation of the rational aspect,

to the detriment of feeling. But now I was able to draw upon my
unconscious — the sea — and recover the dimension I had neglected,
here symbolized by flowers, which commonly represent emotion and
feeling as opposed to rationality.

Let us now look at the dream Arion brought to our final session:

> As I enter my house, I see my face in a mirror. I am surprised by the
> heightened, almost suntanned color, which makes me look more alive
> and even more attractive. I take off my glasses and go closer to the
> mirror, struck by the change in my eyes: they are clearer, purer, more
> expressive. I have never seen them this way and think that it must be a
> real metamorphosis.

Notice first of all that the dreamer looks at himself in a mirror.
This image, on which Jacques Lacan bases his psychological theories,[152] implies the possibility of recognizing oneself: the mirror in
fact gives us back our reality. The dreamer sees himself as tanned; his
skin has therefore been exposed to the sun, which in myths always
stands for the source of life and light. The years of psychological
work have "enlightened" him, allowed him to understand much about
himself, and at this point he can even look at himself "without
glasses." This detail recalls a previous dream, in which he perceived
the face of the woman he loved on the other side of a window frosted
with ice (above, page 78). We interpreted his careful and patient cleaning of those windowpanes as the process of withdrawing his projections, and now we can see in the removal of his glasses the possibility
of observing *himself* consciously and without veils. And here a miracle occurs: he sees the change in his eyes, which are clear and pure.

The eye, the mirror of the soul even in common parlance, is charged
with profound psychological meaning. It is easy to observe how two
persons can look each other in the eye, without feeling an inexplic-
able anxiety, only if a deep bond exists between them. And it is the
same with oneself: the dreamer can look fearlessly into his own eyes
because his relations with his interiority have changed. And at this
point his relation to the analyst and the analyst's interpretations has
also changed; looking honestly into his own eyes expresses, in short,
the search for individual solutions to that problem that each person
constitutes for himself, and for which no one else can provide valid
answers. An analysis that has "taken" should lead precisely to this.
If the patient were to go away with *my* view of the world, nothing
would have happened except suggestion, not analysis. The latter means

in fact to place the other in a position to use an instrument that he already possesses: the capacity to recognize an individual truth within himself.

All the myriad answers that have been given to the problems of man, the "great" books that have been written, have surely emerged from the depths of their authors and from the relation they endured with themselves. But even if their answers are to some extent universally valid, it will never be sufficient to read and learn them, for they will still express "their" truth and not ours. As Jung says:

> The needful thing is not to *know* the truth but to *experience* it. Not to have an intellectual conception of things, but to find our way to the inner, and perhaps wordless, irrational experience — that is the great problem.[153]

My task as analyst is to help the other to look inside himself, to assist him in his search, without suggesting any sort of answers, since I really do not have answers to give him. His suffering is absolutely personal, and so must be the solution. The patient must therefore make a leap: he must give up the answers he has absorbed from religion, philosophy or politics, and ask of *himself* the meaning of what is troubling him. He must learn to listen to what is communicated to him by his own suffering and learn to translate it into a language of *his own* that will also express *his* philosophy. Then he will also find that where someone else has experienced and expressed the same things, he is able to appreciate all the more their words because they will find a genuine echo within himself. Indeed, the boundary to our subjectivity lies in an objectivity of the psyche that we cannot help recognizing behind the most diverse manifestations. And it is for this reason that individuation does not mean individualism, but rather a deeper, because conscious, contact with the common human dimension.[154]

From this standpoint, analysis is not the treatment of a symptom but the reconstruction of an individuality wherein the irrational factors that are the foundation of man find their place. With this in mind, as Jung says:

> Psychotherapy . . . ceases to be merely a method for treating the sick. It now treats the healthy or such as have a moral right to psychic health, whose sickness is at most the suffering that torments us all.[155]

And when the patient understands this, it is time to take leave of each other. The words I say to him at the moment of parting are not reassurance, but a recognition of his individuality and otherness. But there is also something that I say to myself, since I realize that my work has been of a "diabolical" nature, in that more inner "demons" have also come to the surface. The analytic process, in fact, does not provide happiness but a more acute awareness of one's own suffering and contradictions. In other words, the person becomes an adult responsible for his own life and can no longer allow himself to ascribe to anyone else the burden of his choices and mistakes. This, however, is the only way we can enter into history and cease to be its passive objects.

The reader will understand at this point how the freedom gained by the patient is closely linked to my own capacity to be a free individual, and how therefore it is not just *one* patient who raises questions about my entire self: in reality every patient allows and obliges the analyst to scrutinize himself and his life. But for this to happen it is necessary, as I said at the beginning, for the analyst not to *play* the analyst but to *be* one, and as such to be a person perennially dissatisfied, forever "wishful" in the presence of every patient. This wish generally coincides with love, understood in the broadest sense of the word. Freud, too, declared that "love is the great educator."[156] It is necessary, however, to understand the circularity or mutuality of the analytic relationship, in which love cannot be one-sided if it truly wants to be effective. If the analyst does not "desire" his patient, the latter will never grow, but of course the opposite is also true. The animal placed by Jorge Luis Borges in the Tower of Victory in Chitor is always in a lethargic state, and "only when someone starts up the spiraling stairs is [it] brought to consciousness."[157] The animal must try to climb to the top of the tower because for it to ascend means to perfect itself, and when the last visitor goes away it falls back to the lowest step. The story adds, however:

> At each level the creature's color becomes more intense, its shape approaches perfection, and the bluish light it gives off is more brilliant. But it achieves its ultimate form only at the topmost step, when the climber is a person who has attained Nirvana and whose acts cast no shadows.[158]

Borges' fantastic tale poetically illuminates the meaning of the analytic "way": a series of absurdities, of apparently pointless sufferings, which have precisely the good fortune to be transformed into a "way"[159] for the patient and the analyst — a way that restores to them their human dignity.

Notes

CW — *The Collected Works of C.G. Jung*, trans. R.F.C. Hull, ed. H. Read, M. Fordham, G. Adler, Wm. McGuire, Bollingen Series XX (Princeton: Princeton University Press, 1953–1979).

SE — *The Standard Edition of the Complete Psychological Works of Sigmund Freud*, trans. James Strachey (London: Hogarth Press, 1964).

1. Juvenal, III.8.85; English translation: *The Sixteen Satires* (Middlesex: Penguin Books, 1980), p. 180.
2. O. Spengler, *The Decline of the West* (New York: Knopf, 1937), vol. 2, p. 212.
3. C.G. Jung, "Psychotherapy and a Philosophy of Life," *The Practice of Psychotherapy*, CW 16, par. 185.
4. Jung, "The Psychology of the Transference," ibid., par. 534.
5. Ibid., par. 364 (italics added).
6. E. Neumann, *The Origins and History of Consciousness*, Bollingen Series XLII, trans. R.F.C. Hull (Princeton: Princeton University Press, 1954).
7. G. Pascoli, *Poemi conviviali* [Festive Poems] (Milan: Mondadori, 1980), p. 243.
8. V. Hugo, *Les Misérables* (Middlesex, Penguin Books, 1982), p. 597.
9. Neumann, *Origins*, pp. 5-38.
10. Ibid., p. 18.
11. Ibid., p. 41. See also James Hillman, *The Myth of Analysis* (Evanston: Northwestern University Press, 1972), pp. 80-83, and *Pan and the Nightmare* (Zurich: Spring Publications, 1972), pp. xxx-xxxi.
12. T. Hoving, *Tutankhamun: The Untold Story* (New York: Simon and Schuster, 1978), p. 369.
13. E. Bernhard, *Mitobiographia* (Milan: Adelphi, 1969).
14. Miguel de Unamuno, *Tragic Sense of Life* (New York: Dover Publications, 1954), p. 18.
15. Franz Kafka, "Reflections on Sin, Pain, Hope, and the True Way," in *The Great Wall of China: Stories and Reflections* (New York: Schocken Books, 1970), p. 164.
16. Neumann, *Origins*, pp. 102-103.
17. E. Cassirer, *The Logic of the Humanities*, trans. Clarence Smith Howe (New Haven: Yale University Press, 1961), pp. 86-116.
18. Ibid., p. 95.

19. Neumann, *Origins*, p. 16.

20. Ibid.

21. Ibid.

22. *Myth, Religion, and Mother Right: Selected Writings of J.J. Bachofen,* trans. Ralph Manheim, Bollingen Series LXXXIV (Princeton, Princeton University Press, 1967), p. 69.

23. Neumann, *Origins*, p. 42.

24. Albert Camus, *The Myth of Sisyphus and Other Essays*, trans. Justin O'Brien (New York: Knopf, 1955), p. 137.

25. Neumann, *Origins*, p. 147.

26. Rainer Maria Rilke, *Letters to a Young Poet*, trans. M.D. Herter Norton, rev. ed. (New York: W.W. Norton, 1954), p. 18.

27. E. Neumann, "Narcissism, Normal Self-Formation, and the Primary Relation to the Mother," in *Spring 1966*, p. 89.

28. Ibid., p. 90.

29. Ibid., p. 87.

30. Jean Rostand, *Pensieri di un biologo* [Reflections of a Biologist] (Milan: Edizioni del Borghese, 1968), p. 87.

31. E. Neumann, *The Archetypal World of Henry Moore*, trans. R.F.C. Hull (New York: Pantheon Books, 1959), pp. 66-67.

32. Sigmund Freud, *The Interpretation of Dreams*, SE 5, p. 398n.

33. Otto Rank, *The Double: A Psychoanalytic Study* (Chapel Hill: University of North Carolina Press, 1971).

34. Freud, "The 'Uncanny,' " SE 17, pp. 219-252.

35. J.G. Frazer, *The Golden Bough: A Study in Magic and Religion*, Part II: "Taboo and the Perils of the Soul," 3rd ed. (New York: Macmillan, 1951), pp. 94-95; see also G. van der Leeuw, *Fenomenologia della religione* [Phenomenology of Religion] (Turin: Boringhieri, 1975), p. 228.

36. Jung, *Mysterium Conjunctionis*, CW 14, par. 756.

37. Hillman, *Myth of Analysis*, p. 81.

38. Thomas Mann, *Joseph and His Brothers*, trans. H.T. Lowe-Porter (New York: Knopf, 1968), p. 78.

39. Freud, "Fixation to Traumas — The Unconscious," *Introductory Lectures on Psycho-Analysis* (Part III), SE 16, p. 285.

40. Jung, "Psychology of the Transference," *The Practice of Psychotherapy*, CW 16, par. 476.

41. Ibid.

42. Jung, "The Psychological Foundations of Belief in Spirits," *The Structure and Dynamics of the Psyche*, CW 8, pars. 587, 594.

43. Neumann, *Origins*, pp. 16-17.

44. Jung, "Psychology of the Transference," *The Practice of Psychotherapy*, CW 16, pars. 477-478.

45. Seneca, *De Ira*, II.XII.3 (Turin: Paravia, 1940), p. 37.

46. Jung, "Forewords to Jung: *Seelenprobleme der Gegenwart*," *The Symbolic Life*, CW 18, par. 1292.

47. H. Melville, *Moby-Dick* (Middlesex: Penguin Books, 1981), p. 243.

48. Neumann, *Origins*, pp. 102-127.

49. Ibid., pp. 114-116.

50. Ibid., p. 123.

51. Ibid., p. 126.

52. Ibid., p. 6.

53. Ibid., p. 126.

54. "Galileo," in *Seven Plays by Bertolt Brecht*, ed. Eric Bentley (New York: Grove Press, 1961), p. 392.

55. G.W.F. Hegel, *The Phenomenology of Mind* (New York: Harper & Row, 1967), p. 74.

56. Freud, "Family Romances," *Jensen's "Gradiva" and Other Works*, SE 9, pp. 237-241.

57. Neumann, *Origins*, p. 135.

58. Ibid., p. 134.

59. Rilke, *Letters to a Young Poet*, pp. 47-48.

60. S. Quasimodo, *Ed è subito sera* [And Suddenly It's Evening] (Milan: Mondadori, 1977), p. 163.

61. Freud, "The Theme of the Three Caskets," SE 12, p. 300.

62. John Blofeld, *The Book of Change* (London: George Allen & Unwin, 1965), p. 197.

63. John Burnet, *Early Greek Philosophy* (New York: World Publishing Co., 1957), p. 140.

64. W.M. Kranefeldt, " 'Komplex' and Mythos," in C.G. Jung and others, *Seelenprobleme der Gegenwart* (Zurich, 1930).

65. Jung, "Analytical Psychology and *Weltanschauung*," *The Structure and Dynamics of the Psyche*, CW 8, par. 740.

66. Quoted in Martin Heidegger, *Essere e tempo* [Being and Time] (Milan: Longanesi, 1970), p. 655n.

67. J. Laplanche and J.B. Pontalis, *Enciclopedia della psicanalisi* [Encyclopedia of Psychoanalysis] (Bari: Leterza, 1968), pp. 42-44.

68. G. Colli, *La nascita della filosofia* [The Birth of Philosophy] (Milan: Adelphi, 1975), p. 29.

69. Hillman, *Myth of Analysis*, p. 109.

70. Ibid.

71. Michel Neyraut, *Le transfert* [The Transference] (Paris: Presses Universitaires de France, 1974), p. 56.

72. Claude Lévi-Strauss, "La struttura e la forma," [Structure and Form] in V. Ja. Propp, *Morfologia della fiaba* [Morphology of Fables] (Turin: Einaudi, 1966), p. 172.

73. E.R. Dodds, *The Greeks and the Irrational* (Berkeley: University of California Press, 1951), pp. 110-116.

74. Neumann, *Origins*, pp. 204-205.

75. Ibid., p. 187.

76. Ibid., pp. 186-187.

77. Ibid., p. 163.

78. A. Gramsci, *Quaderni dal carcere* [Prison Notebooks], 4 vols. (Turin: Einaudi, 1975), and *Lettere dal carcere* [Letters from Prison] (Turin: Einaudi, 1975).

79. Gramsci, *Lettere*, p. 310.

80. Aeschylus, *The Oresteia* (New York: Bantam Books, 1977), p. 143; see also Melanie Klein, "Some Reflections on *The Oresteia*," in *Envy and Gratitude & Other Works, 1946-1963* (London: Delacorte Press, 1975), p. 281.

81. C. Dossi, *Note azzurre* [Blue Notes] (Milan: Adelphi, 1964), vol 1, p. 499.

82. F. Dostoyevsky, *Pensieri* [Thoughts], comp. and trans. Eva Amendola (Rome: Bocca, 1956), p. 43.

83. John 3:21.

84. W. Goethe, *Teoria della natura* [Theory of Nature] (Turin: Boringhieri, 1958), p. 137.

85. H.F. Ellenberger, *The Discovery of the Unconscious: The History and Evolution of Dynamic Psychiatry* (New York: Basic Books, 1970), p. 267.

86. F. Nietzsche, *The Gay Science*, trans. Walter Kaufmann (New York: Vintage Books, 1974), p. 219.

87. Klein, *Envy and Gratitude*, pp. 176-235. See also Ann and Barry Ulanov, *Cinderella and Her Sisters: The Envied and the Envying* (Philadelphia: The Westminster Press, 1983).

88. James Hillman, "Inner Life: The Unconscious as Experience," in *Insearch: Psychology and Religion* (New York: Charles Scribner's Sons, 1967), p. 43.

89. Jung, *Psychological Types*, CW 6, par. 844.

90. Neumann, *Origins*, p. 165.

91. Ibid., pp. 172-173.

92. R.W. Clark, *Einstein: The Life and Times* (London: Hodder and Stoughton, 1973), p. 443.

93. Neumann, *Origins*, p. 184.

94. Ibid., p. 171.

95. E. Neumann, "Creative Man and Transformation," *Art and the Creative Unconscious* (New York: Pantheon Books, 1959), pp. 149-205.

96. Colli, *La nascita della filosofia*, p. 53.

97. Jung, "The Relations between the Ego and the Unconscious," *Two Essays*, CW 7, par. 254.

98. J. Monod, *Chance and Necessity*, trans. Austryn Wainhouse (New York: Vintage Books, 1971).

99. Jung, *Psychology and Alchemy*, CW 12, par. 24.

100. G.W.F. Hegel, *Phenomenology of Mind*, p. 74.

101. Leonardo da Vinci, *Scritti letterari* [Literary Writings] (Milan: Rizzoli, 1974), p. 67.

102. W.H. Auden, quoted in E.R. Dodds, *Pagan and Christian in an Age of Anxiety* (New York: W.W. Norton, 1970), p. 37.

103. Jung, "Archetypes of the Collective Unconscious," *The Archetypes and the Collective Unconscious*, CW 9i, par. 66.

104. Bernhard, *Mitobiografia*, pp. 136-137.

105. Jung, "Psychology of the Transference," *The Practice of Psychotherapy*, CW 16, pars. 444-445.

106. F. Nietzsche, *Umano, troppo umano* [Human, All Too Human] (Milan: Adelphi, 1977), p. 325.

107. Jung, "Psychotherapists or the Clergy," *Psychology and Religion: West and East*, CW 11, par. 532.

108. Jung, *Psychological Types*, CW 6, par. 84.

109. Jung, "Psychotherapists or the Clergy," *Psychology and Religion*, CW 11, par. 534.

110. J.W. Perry, *The Far Side of Madness* (Englewood Cliffs: Prentice-Hall, 1974).

111. Bernhard, *Mitobiografia*, p. 138.

112. S. Kierkegaard, *Either/Or* (Princeton: Princeton University Press, 1971), vol. 1, p. 74.

113. Jung, "The Relations between the Ego and the Unconscious," *Two Essays on Analytical Psychology*, CW 7, par. 210.

114. Jung, "Fundamental Questions of Psychotherapy," *The Practice of Psychotherapy*, CW 16, par. 236 (italics added).

115. Edward C. Whitmont, "Reassessing Feminity and Masculinity: A Critique of Some Traditional Assumptions," in *Money, Food, Drink, Fash-*

ion and Analytic Training: Depth Dimensions of Physical Existence. Proceedings of the Eighth International Congress for Analytical Psychology, ed. John Beebe (Felbach: Bonz, 1983), pp. 419-431.

116. Neumann, *Origins*, p. 220.

117. Ibid.

118. Ibid., p. 221.

119. Jung, "The Real and Surreal," *The Structure and Dynamics of the Psyche*, CW 8, par. 747.

120. Jung, "On the Nature of the Psyche," ibid., par. 425.

121. Jung, "Analytical Psychology and *Weltanschauung*," ibid., par. 707 (italics added).

122. Rainer Maria Rilke, "Il libro della poverta e della morte," [The Book of Poverty and Death], *Liriche e prose* [Poetry and Prose] (Florence: Sansoni, 1968), p. 212.

123. Jung, "Problems of Modern Psychotherapy," *The Practice of Psychotherapy*, CW 16, par. 160.

124. Ibid., p. 70.

125. Albert Einstein, *The Human Side: New Glimpses from His Archives*, eds. H. Dukas and B. Hoffman (Princeton: Princeton University Press, 1979), p. 115.

126. N. Machiavelli, *Pensieri* [Thoughts] (Turin: Fogola Editore, 1980), p. 12.

127. Colli, *La nascita della filosofia*, p. 20.

128. Ibid, p. 21.

129. Ibid., p. 43.

130. E.G. Humbert, "Il ruolo dell'immagine nella psicologia analitica" [The Role of the Imagination in Analytical Psychology], *Rivista di psicologia analitica*, 20/79, p. 15.

131. Jung, *Memories, Dreams, Reflections*, trans. Richard and Clara Winston, ed. Aniela Jaffé (New York: Vintage Books, 1965), p. 187.

132. Jung, "Psychological Factors Determining Human Behavior," *The Structure and Dynamics of the Psyche*, CW 8, par. 241.

133. Jung, *Memories, Dreams, Reflections*, p. 187.

134. Jung, "Problems of Modern Psychotherapy," *The Practice of Psychotherapy*, CW 16, pars. 163, 167.

135. Neumann, *Origins*, p. 325.

136. Ibid. p. 328.

137. Ibid., p. 336.

138. Ibid., p. 339.

139. Jung, *Two Essays*, CW 7, pars. 206-209.

140. Neumann, *Origins*, p. 335.

141. Jung, *Memories, Dreams, Reflections*, p. 325.

142. Max Weber, *The Protestant Ethic and the Spirit of Capitalism* (New York: Scribner, 1948).

143. Jung, "Archetypes of the Collective Unconscious," *The Archetypes and the Collective Unconscious*, CW 9i, par. 66.

144. Neumann, *Origins*, p. 286.

145. Jung, *Psychological Types*, CW 6, par. 105.

146. Ibid., par. 109.

147. Ibid., pars. 78, 80.

148. Ibid., par. 93.

149. Neumann, *Origins*, p. 340.

150. Jung, *Memories, Dreams, Reflections*, p. 344.

151. Rilke, *Letters to a Young Poet*, p. 69.

152. J. Lacan, *Ecrits: A Selection*, trans. Alan Sheridan (New York: W.W. Norton, 1977), pp. 1-7.

153. Jung, "Forewords to Jung: *Seelenprobleme der Gegenwart*," *The Symbolic Life*, CW 18, par. 1292.

154. For an overview of Jung's idea of individuation, see, "The Relations between the Ego and the Unconscious," *Two Essays*, CW 7, pars. 266-269; "Definitions," *Psychological Types*, CW 6, pars. 757-762; and "On the Nature of the Psyche," *The Structure and Dynamics of the Psyche*, CW 8, par. 432. See also Miguel Serrano, *C.G. Jung and Hermann Hesse: A Record of Two Friendships*, trans. Frank MacShane (London: Routledge & Kegan Paul, 1966).

155. Jung, "Problems of Modern Psychotherapy," *The Practice of Psychotherapy*, CW 16, par. 174.

156. Freud, "Some Character-Types Met with in Psycho-Analytic Work," SE 14, p. 312.

157. J.L. Borges (with Margarita Guerrero), "A Bao A Qu," in *The Book of Imaginary Beings*, trans. Norman Thomas di Giovanni (New York: Dutton, 1978), p. 21.

158. Ibid.

159. E. Neumann, *Amor and Psyche: The Psychic Development of the Feminine*, Bollingen Series LIV, trans. Ralph Manheim (Princeton: Princeton University Press, 1956), p. 98.

Glossary of Jungian Terms

Anima (Latin, "soul"). The unconscious, feminine side of a man's personality. She is personified in dreams by images of women ranging from prostitute and seductress to spiritual guide (Wisdom). She is the eros principle, hence a man's anima development is reflected in how he relates to women. Identification with the anima can appear as moodiness, effeminacy, and oversensitivity. Jung calls the anima *the archetype of life itself.*

Animus (Latin, "spirit"). The unconscious, masculine side of a woman's personality. He personifies the logos principle. Identification with the animus can cause a woman to become rigid, opinionated, and argumentative. More positively, he is the inner man who acts as a bridge between the woman's ego and her own creative resources in the unconscious.

Archetypes. Irrepresentable in themselves, but their effects appear in consciousness as the archetypal images and ideas. These are universal patterns or motifs which come from the collective unconscious and are the basic content of religions, mythologies, legends, and fairytales. They emerge in individuals through dreams and visions.

Association. A spontaneous flow of interconnected thoughts and images around a specific idea, determined by unconscious connections.

Complex. An emotionally charged group of ideas or images. At the "center" of a complex is an archetype or archetypal image.

Constellate. Whenever there is a strong emotional reaction to a person or a situation, a complex has been constellated (activated).

Ego. The central complex in the field of consciousness. A strong ego can relate objectively to activated contents of the unconscious (i.e., other complexes), rather than identifying with them, which appears as a state of possession.

Feeling. One of the four psychic functions. It is a rational function which evaluates the worth of relationships and situations. Feeling must be distinguished from emotion, which is due to an activated complex.

Individuation. The conscious realization of one's unique psychological reality, including both strengths and limitations. It leads to the experience of the Self as the regulating center of the psyche.

Inflation. A state in which one has an unrealistically high or low (negative inflation) sense of identity. It indicates a regression of consciousness into unconsciousness, which typically happens when the ego takes too many unconscious contents upon itself and loses the faculty of discrimination.

Intuition. One of the four psychic functions. It is the irrational function which tells us the possibilities inherent in the present. In contrast to sensation (the function which perceives immediate reality through the physical senses) intuition perceives via the unconscious, e.g., flashes of insight of unknown origin.

Participation mystique. A term derived from the anthropologist Lévy-Bruhl, denoting a primitive, psychological connection with objects, or between persons, resulting in a strong unconscious bond.

Persona (Latin, "actor's mask"). One's social role, derived from the expectations of society and early training. A strong ego relates to the outside world through a flexible persona; identification with a specific persona (doctor, scholar, artist, etc.) inhibits psychological development.

Projection. The process whereby an unconscious quality or characteristic of one's own is perceived and reacted to in an outer object or person. Projection of the anima or animus onto a real women or man is experienced as falling in love. Frustrated expectations indicate the need to withdraw projections, in order to relate to the reality of other people.

Puer aeternus (Latin, "eternal youth"). Indicates a certain type of man who remains too long in adolescent psychology, generally associated with a strong unconscious attachment to the mother (actual or symbolic). Positive traits are spontaneity and openness to change. His female counterpart is the **puella,** an "eternal girl" with a corresponding attachment to the father-world.

Self. The archetype of wholeness and the regulating center of the personality. It is experienced as a transpersonal power which transcends the ego, e.g., God.

Senex (Latin, "old man"). Associated with attitudes that come with advancing age. Negatively, this can mean cynicism, rigidity and extreme conservatism; positive traits are responsibility, orderliness and self-discipline. A well-balanced personality functions appropriately within the puer-senex polarity.

Shadow. An unconscious part of the personality characterized by traits and attitudes, whether negative or positive, which the conscious ego tends to reject or ignore. It is personified in dreams by persons of the same sex as the dreamer. Consciously assimilating one's shadow usually results in an increase of energy.

Symbol. The best possible expression for something essentially unknown. Symbolic thinking is non-linear, right-brain oriented; it is complementary to logical, linear, left-brain thinking.

Transcendent function. The reconciling "third" which emerges from the unconscious (in the form of a symbol or a new attitude) after the conflicting opposites have been consciously differentiated, and the tension between them held.

Transference and countertransference. Particular cases of projection, commonly used to describe the unconscious, emotional bonds that arise between two persons in an analytic or therapeutic relationship.

Uroboros. The mythical snake or dragon that eats its own tail. It is a symbol both for individuation as a self-contained, circular process, and for narcissistic self-absorption.

Index

abstraction, 113-114
Adam and Eve, 19
action, and analysis, 74-76, 82-85,
  87-88, 105, 107-108
adolescence, 36-37, 56, 70-71, 87,
  90-91, 115
Aeschylus, 63
Agamemnon, 61
aggression, 62, 90, 92-95, 98,
  120-121
alimentary symbolism, 37-38
alter ego, 25-29
ambivalence, 35-37, 54-55, 109
analysis: 8-19, 25-29, 31-36,
  40-44, 45-56, 58-59, 64,
  74-79, 87-88, 91, 93-95, 98,
  101-104, 110, 117, 121-125
  and action, 74-76, 82-85, 87-88,
  105, 107-108
  reductive, 9, 14, 16, 37, 54-56,
  66, 82
analytic relationship: 8-12, 22,
  25-29, 33-35, 64-66, 82, 85,
  88, 101-102, 107-108, 114,
  117-118, 121-125
  and love, 16, 34, 49, 125
Andersen, Hans Christian, 83
androgyny, 39
anima: 51-52, 76-86, 93, 105, 110,
  116, 118, 120
  as inner treasure, 51-52, 76-77
  and outer woman, 50-52, 76-89,
  105-106, 114, 116-117
animus: 51-52, 81
  as prince, 83
archetypes/archetypal images: 9-10,
  13-14, 24, 45, 48, 68-73,
  81-85, 89-91, 94-95, 118
  fragmentation of, 109-110,
  112-114
  possession by, 113-114

Ariadne, 49-51
Auden, W.H., 76
automorphism, 23

Bachofen, J.J., 20-21
Bernhard, E., 82, 87, 92
bicycle, in dream, 32
biting, 37
Borges, Jorge Luis, 125
Brecht, B., 40
Bruno, Giordano, 62
Buber, Martin, 116
Buddha, 96

Camus, Albert, 20
cannibalism, in dream, 67-68
capitalism, 116
carpenter, in dream, 102
castration, 54, 66-67, 87
caves, in dream, 11-13
cellar, in dream, 104
centroversion, 96-97, 119-120
Cerberus, 55
charity, 46
Christ/Christianity, 41, 73, 89,
  96-99, 111
cleaning, in dream, 78-79
collective: as father world, 56-57,
  68-73
  versus individual, 14-15, 19,
  41-42, 68-73, 96-97, 106-107,
  111, 113
Colli, G., 49, 71
communication, intersubjective, 29
complexes, 79, 88
conflict: absence of, 12, 20, 77
  between generations, 70-71
  importance of, 12, 21, 23-29,
  31-32, 35, 62-63, 70-71, 73,
  91-93, 95, 107-108
Confucius, 13

Studies in Jungian Psychology
by Jungian Analysts

LIMITED EDITION PAPERBACKS

Prices quoted are in U.S. dollars (except for Canadian orders)

1. **The Secret Raven: Conflict and Transformation.**
   Daryl Sharp (Toronto). ISBN 0-919123-00-7. 128 pages. $10

A concise introduction to the application of Jungian psychology. Focuses on the creative personality—and the life and dreams of the writer Franz Kafka—but the psychology is relevant to anyone who has experienced a conflict between the spiritual life and sex, or between inner and outer reality. (Knowledge of Kafka is not necessary.) Illustrated. Bibliography.

2. **The Psychological Meaning of Redemption Motifs in Fairytales.**
   Marie-Louise von Franz (Zurich). ISBN 0-919123-01-5. 128 pages. $10

A unique account of the significance of fairytales for an understanding of the process of individuation, especially in terms of integrating animal nature and human nature. Particularly helpful for its symbolic, nonlinear approach to the meaning of typical dream motifs (bathing, beating, clothes, animals, etc.), and its clear description of complexes and projection.

3. **On Divination and Synchronicity: Psychology of Meaningful Chance.**
   Marie-Louise von Franz (Zurich). ISBN 0-919123-02-3. 128 pages. $10

A penetrating study of the meaning of the irrational. Examines time, number, and methods of divining fate such as the I Ching, astrology, Tarot, palmistry, random patterns, etc. Explains Jung's ideas on archetypes, projection, psychic energy and synchronicity, contrasting Western scientific attitudes with those of the Chinese and so-called primitives. Illustrated.

4. **The Owl Was a Baker's Daughter: Obesity, Anorexia Nervosa, and the Repressed Feminine.**
   Marion Woodman (Toronto). ISBN 0-919123-03-1. 144 pages. $10

A pioneer work in feminine psychology, with particular attention to the body as mirror of the psyche in eating disorders and weight disturbances. Explores the personal and cultural loss—and potential rediscovery—of the feminine principle, through Jung's Association Experiment, case studies, dreams, Christianity and mythology. Illustrated. Glossary. Bibliography.

5. **Alchemy: An Introduction to the Symbolism and the Psychology.**
   Marie-Louise von Franz (Zurich). ISBN 0-919123-04-X. 288 pages. $16

A lucid and practical guide to what the alchemists were really looking for—emotional balance and wholeness. Completely demystifies the subject. An important work, invaluable for an understanding of images and motifs in modern dreams and drawings, and indispensable for anyone interested in relationships and communication between the sexes. 84 Illustrations.

6. **Descent to the Goddess: A Way of Initiation for Women.**
   Sylvia Brinton Perera (New York). ISBN 0-919123-05-8. 112 pages. $10

A timely and provocative study of women's freedom and the need for an inner, female authority in a masculine-oriented society. Based on the Sumerian goddess Inanna-Ishtar's journey to the underworld, her transformation through contact with her dark "sister" Ereshkigal, and her return. Rich in insights from dreams, mythology and analysis. Glossary. Bibliography.

7. The Psyche as Sacrament: C.G. Jung and Paul Tillich.
John P. Dourley (Ottawa). ISBN 0-919123-06-6. 128 pages. $10

An illuminating, comparative study showing with great clarity that in the depths of the soul the psychological task and the religious task are one. With a dual perspective, the author—Jungian analyst and Catholic priest—examines the deeper meaning, for Christian and non-Christian alike, of God, Christ, the Spirit, the Trinity, morality and the religious life. Glossary.

8. Border Crossings: Carlos Castaneda's Path of Knowledge.
Donald Lee Williams (Boulder). ISBN 0-919123-07-4. 160 pages. $12

The first thorough psychological examination of the popular don Juan novels. Using dreams, fairytales, and mythic and cultural parallels, the author brings Castaneda's spiritual journey down to earth, in terms of everyone's search for self-realization. Special attention to the psychology of women. (Familiarity with the novels is not necessary.) Glossary.

9. Narcissism and Character Transformation: The Psychology of Narcissistic Character Disorders.
Nathan Schwartz-Salant (New York). ISBN 0-919123-08-2. 192 pp. $13

An incisive and comprehensive analysis of narcissism: what it looks like, what it means and how to deal with it. Shows how an understanding of the archetypal patterns that underlie the individual, clinical symptoms of narcissism can point the way to a healthy restructuring of the personality. Draws upon a variety of psychoanalytic points of view (Jungian, Freudian, Kohutian, Kleinian, etc.). Illustrated. Glossary. Bibliography.

10. Rape and Ritual: A Psychological Study.
Bradley A. Te Paske (Minneapolis). ISBN 0-919123-09-0. 160 pp. $12

An absorbing combination of theory, clinical material, dreams and mythology, penetrating far beyond the actual deed to the impersonal, archetypal background of sexual assault. Special attention to male ambivalence toward women and the psychological significance of rape dreams and fantasies. Illustrated. Glossary. Bibliography.

11. Alcoholism and Women: The Background and the Psychology.
Jan Bauer (Zurich). ISBN 0-919123-10-4. 144 pages. $12

A major contribution to an understanding of alcoholism, particularly in women. Compares and contrasts medical and psychological models, illustrates the relative merits of Alcoholics Anonymous and individual therapy, and presents new ways of looking at the problem based on case material, dreams and archetypal patterns. Glossary. Bibliography.

12. Addiction to Perfection: The Still Unravished Bride.
Marion Woodman (Toronto). ISBN 0-919123-11-2. 208 pages. $12

A powerful and authoritative look at the psychology and attitudes of modern woman, expanding on the themes introduced in *The Owl Was a Baker's Daughter*. Explores the nature of the feminine through case material, dreams and mythology, in food rituals, rape symbolism, perfectionism, imagery in the body, sexuality and creativity. Illustrated.

13. Jungian Dream Interpretation: A Handbook of Theory and Practice.
James A. Hall, M.D. (Dallas). ISBN 0-919123-12-0. 128 pages. $12

A comprehensive and practical guide to an understanding of dreams in light of the basic concepts of Jungian psychology. Jung's model of the psyche is described and discussed, with many clinical examples. Particular attention to common dream motifs, and how dreams are related to the stage of life and individuation process of the dreamer. Glossary.

14. The Creation of Consciousness: Jung's Myth for Modern Man.
Edward F. Edinger, M.D. (Los Angeles). ISBN 0-919123-13-9. 128 pp. $12

An important new book by the author of *Ego and Archetype,* proposing a world-view based on a creative collaboration between the scientific pursuit of knowledge and the religious search for meaning. Explores the significance of Jung's life and work, the meaning of human life and the pressing need for humanity to become conscious of its dark, destructive side. Illustrated.

15. The Analytic Encounter: Transference and Human Relationship.
Mario Jacoby (Zurich). ISBN 0-919123-14-7. 128 pp. $12

A sensitive study illustrating the difference between relationships based on projection and those characterized by psychological objectivity and mutual respect. Examines the views of Jung, Freud and Martin Buber, with special attention to the purpose of projection. Illustrated. Glossary. Bibliography.

16. Change of Life: Dreams and the Menopause.
Ann Mankowitz (Santa Fe). ISBN 0-919123-15-5. 128 pp. $12

A moving account of a menopausal woman's Jungian analysis, dramatically interweaving the experience of one woman with generally applicable social, biological, emotional and psychological factors. Frankly discusses the realities of aging, revealing the menopause as a time of rebirth, an opportunity for increased strength and specifically feminine wisdom. Bibliography.

17. The Illness That We Are: A Jungian Critique of Christianity.
John P. Dourley (Ottawa). ISBN 0-919123-16-3. 128 pp. $12

A radical study by Catholic priest and analyst, exploring the strengths and weaknesses of the Christian myth in terms of the psychological and religious search for wholeness. Special attention to Jung's views that the Gnostic, mystical and alchemical traditions contain the necessary compensation for the essentially extraverted and masculine ideals of Christianity.

18. Hags and Heroes: A Feminist Approach to Jungian Psychotherapy with Couples. ISBN 0-919123-17-1. 192 pp. $14
Polly Young-Eisendrath (Philadelphia)

A highly original contribution to couple therapy, integrating feminist views with the concepts of Jung and Harry Stack Sullivan. A wealth of helpful guidelines for both therapists and clients, including detailed suggestions for psychosexual and developmental assessment. Emphasis on revaluing the feminine and re-assessing the nature of female authority. Bibliography.

19. Cultural Attitudes in Psychological Perspective. 128 pp. $12
Joseph L. Henderson, M.D. (San Francisco). ISBN 0-919123-18-X.

A thoughtful new work by the author of *Thresholds of Initiation* and co-author of *Man and His Symbols.* Examines the nature and value of social, religious, aesthetic and philosophic attitudes, showing how the concepts of analytical psychology can give depth and substance to an individual *Weltanschauung* or world view. Illustrated. Bibliography.

Add $1 per book (bookpost) or $3 per book (airmail)

INNER CITY BOOKS
Box 1271, Station Q, Toronto, Canada M4T 2P4